The Beacon Guide to

New England

Houses of Worship

D0167736

An Architectural Companion

The Beacon Guide to

New England

Houses of Worship

G.E. Kidder Smith

Beacon Press · Boston

Beacon Press
25 Beacon Street
Boston, Massachusetts 02108-2800

Beacon Press books
are published under the auspices of
the Unitarian Universalist Association of Congregations.

96 95 94 93 92 91 90 89   8 7 6 5 4 3 2 1
Library of Congress Cataloging-in-Publication Data
Smith, G. E. (George Everard)
    The Beacon guide to New England houses of worship / G. E. Kidder
Smith   p. cm.
    Includes bibliographical references and index.
    ISBN 0-8070-5101-2
    1. Church architecture—New England—Guide-books.   2. New England—
Description and travel—Guide-books.   I. Title
NA5215.S6   1989
917.4'0443—dc   19   89-31276

G. E. Kidder Smith is a Fellow of the American Institute of Architects, a
noted architectural critic and photographer, and author of the three-volume
guide, *The Architecture of the United States.*

For Kidder and Hoppy

CONTENTS

The white-steepled New England Church, set alternatively amid dazzling snow or brilliantly colored autumn leaves, evokes a beloved picture in the American imagination—equaled as an image of the New World environment only by the New York skyline or an old snapshot of some western "Main Street." On the global scale of religious buildings, the New England church would win the popularity contest for America along with the cathedral for Europe and the pagoda for Japan. We are dealing here not only with a major chapter in the history of world architecture, but one which is as genuinely loved by the public as it is respected and researched by scholars and architectural historians.

So Kidder Smith's guidebook pulls the strings of an architectural heartland for today, just as *Brazil Builds,* which he did with Philip L. Goodwin, established a new frontier of architectural sophistication for American readers in 1943.

Beyond dealing with a favorite subject, however, this book breaks important ground in two unexpected directions. First, it really delivers what its title proclaims: houses of worship in New England, not just white steeples. Of the one hundred buildings described and photographed by Mr. Kidder Smith, thirty-six are "Colonial," forty Federal/Greek Revival, eleven Gothic Revival/Victorian, and *mirabile dictu,* thirteen modern. The religious spectrum is covered as well: Congregational, Unitarian Universalist, Episcopal, Roman Catholic, nondenominational, Jewish, Baptist, Shaker, Methodist, Presbyterian, Lutheran, Quaker.

Of course the lion's share are Congregational and Unitarian Universalist churches (sixty-three in total) because that's just how the numbers fall out, but the equally important fact to remember is that America's earliest (and probably finest) synagogue and Baptist church are in Newport and Providence; that arguably the most important Episcopal treasure is H. H. Richardson's Trinity Church in Boston; and that two of the best modern churches anywhere are Saarinen's chapel at MIT and Wallace Harrison's First Presbyterian Church in Stamford.

Which leads me to the second sleeper about this book: although the Puritan meetinghouses and endlessly varied white steeples of Colonial and Greek Revival design are the undisputed flagships of this stately procession, the quality and variety of later nineteenth- and twentieth-century houses of worship make New England a microcosm for the study of *all* religious architecture in America. Apart from the one obvious lacuna of the Spanish baroque mission churches of the Southwest, everything else is here, and here in extraordinary strength. In short—thanks to the author's selection of examples, the written analysis in which he connects and contrasts the stylistic development from one church to the next, and, finally, the description of the liturgical and broader cultural requirements of the various religious traditions—we have here an eminently accessible history of American sacred architecture as well as of American religion.

As the reader goes from state to state and church to church, let me forewarn both browser and impatient sleuth alike: do not miss the following seven sacred caches of rare jewels:

- The earliest steeple-less Puritan meetinghouses (Old Ship, Hingham, Mass., [48]; Danville and Sandown, N.H. [67, 78]; Rockingham, Vt. [99]) and the transition to longitudinal churches with towers—West Barnstable, Mass. (63) and particularly Old South, Boston (37), where this process is described in detail. Note also the double doors for men and women in the Shaker and Quaker meetinghouses of Hancock, Mass. (53), Sabbathday Lake, Me. (32), and Dover, N.H. (68), and the former's great open spaces for dancing.

■ The influence of English models in stone—Christopher Wren, James Gibbs, and William Kent in particular—as they are translated into glistening white American wood construction: note especially the towers and porticos of David Hoadley in Avon, Cheshire, Milford, and New Haven, Conn. (1,3,13,15), and his influence in Farmington and Litchfield (4,10). The highest praise for an early American architect, though English born, probably goes to Peter Harrison for his famous trio of King's Chapel, Boston (38), Christ Church, Cambridge (42), and the Touro Synagogue in Newport (85). Paul Revere's Old North Church in Boston (36) is wonderfully described—also its influence on the sister Anglican church of Trinity, Newport (84).

■ Another transition, now from Colonial to Federal/Greek Revival is helpfully analyzed in the Congregational churches in Madison and Meriden, Conn. (11, 12), and celebrated in great detail in Charles Bulfinch's church in Lancaster, Mass. (49). Beyond these, my favorite essays in pure geometry are in the playful towers derived from local builder's copybooks, especially Asher Benjamin's *The Country Builder's Assistant*. What wonderful simple churches in Middlebury and Newfane, Vt. (95, 96), and in Simsbury, Conn. (20), and Provincetown, Mass. (54). Also, don't overlook Elias Carter's three churches in Massachusetts and New Hampshire (51, 69, 71).

■ Luminescent interiors; cove ceilings; elegant raised pulpits; fine chandeliers. See especially the pulpits at Litchfield, Newburyport, and First Unitarian in Providence (9, 52, 89), and the superb interiors of Old North and King's Chapel in Boston (36, 38). But Kidder Smith reserves his highest praise for the stark clarity of the early meetinghouses, such as Amesbury, Mass. (35), and Sandown, N.H. (78), and above all for their translation into the luminosity of Lavius Fillmore's First Congregational Church in Old Bennington, Vt. (97). Here the fullness of the early New England inheritance is fully present.

- Extraordinary groupings of churches, and the felicitous relation of churches and contemporaneous civic buildings in public spaces, is a surprising and most welcome fascination of this book. Mr. Kidder Smith's attention to the famous triad on the New Haven Green is noteworthy, and indeed, Ithiel Town's twin 1814 Gibbsian Congregational and 1815 neo-Gothic Episcopal churches (14, 16), along with Hoadley's United Church (15), form an unprecedented threesome. Note as well the fine composite settings in Sturbridge, Mass. (58), in Temple and Washington, N.H. (80, 81), and in Newfane, Vt. (96).

- Two absolute gems of the Gothic Revival in Maine merit special attention: Anthony Raymond's fantastic (indeed, almost Mannerist, in the tradition of Vanbrugh) Winter Street Church in Bath (24) and the graceful ogee doorway of the Elijah Kellogg church in Harpswell Center (27). Kidder Smith pays important Gothic tribute as well in his careful analysis of the four works of Upjohn (17, 25, 65, 83). His writing about Ralph Adams Cram's influence on American sacred architecture is one of the best parts of the book, and his analysis of Richardson's Trinity Church (39) is a critical high-water mark of appreciation for one of our country's greatest masterpieces.

■ Finally, contemporary architecture is served most wonderfully by Mr. Kidder Smith's detailed description of the one truly transcendent modern church in America, Eero Saarinen's interdenominational chapel at MIT in Cambridge, Mass. (43). Don't miss this.

What a feast! With immense gratitude to Kidder Smith as our guide, let us begin the pilgrimage at once!

The Very Reverend James Parks Morton
Dean, the Cathedral Church of
St. John the Divine

INTRODUCTION

G. E. Kidder Smith

The tidy peninsula known as New England has played a unique role in the development, indeed the alchemy, of the transformation of English colonies into American states. With its seaports closest to Europe and its western edge semi-defined by mountains, New England—so named by Captain John Smith—evolved an ethnic and religious cohesiveness no other section of the nation can match. Among the delights of this religion-spawned, hard-working corner of this country are its picturesque villages and its harmonious houses of worship—meetinghouses, churches, and America's oldest still-standing synagogue. Their architectural responses are of enormous appeal.

It is helpful to keep in mind that the area of all six New England states combined—Maine alone counting for half—is smaller than that of many single Western states. Founded on religious freedom—for its own citizens—New England for well over a century developed a pious population with a disciplined work ethic which enabled it to deal successfully with a difficult climate and obdurate soil. Probably over 90 percent of the early male inhabitants were yeomen, combining farming self-reliance with religious conviction.

The Plymouth Colony Pilgrims (Congregationalists) from their establishment in 1620 to their merger with the Massachusetts Bay Colony Puritans in 1692 formed a rigid theocratic state—one that showed all the intolerance of the liberated. Religion was not a casual affair: Sunday church attendance was required for all—under penalty—often twice on the Sabbath when two-hour sermons in unheated meetinghouses were not uncommon. Heresy was a serious crime, while drunkenness and even games of chance were penal offenses. Roger Williams, the famous liberal, had to flee Massachusetts in 1635 because of his views, escaping to found Rhode Island and to establish religious freedom for all. Salem's so-called witches were hanged in 1692.

From this background came the paradoxical freedom-seeking, freedom-denying Puritans. As life, work, and religion were intertwined, so also were their unique meetinghouses far more than places of worship: they were also the focus of the political and social life of the village. As the communities across New England were basically self-governing, the meetinghouse (a term apparently unknown in England) was of strategic importance, often leading to ugly court battles to determine which "church" would receive taxes and appoint officials. Nor was this conjunction of political and religious functions a short-lived seventeenth-century affair. Even after the Declaration of Independence had dissolved the union of church and state as unconstitutional, New England only reluctantly complied, Massachusetts not separating the two until 1821. Town activities often continued in the meetinghouse long after religious functions left. (It is likely that the seventeenth-century English were glad to have gotten rid of these pesky colonists.)

The architecture of New England, like that in all the thirteen colonies, was naturally influenced by England itself for some two hundred years. This does not mean, however, that the needs and materials of the six New England states did not fashion their own building interpretations, usually on a modest scale. Although Virginia and the Southern colonies extensively employed brick (Williamsburg's elegant series of brick buildings dates from the early 1700s on) New England basically relied on wood. Western Europe had largely exhausted its own timberland by 1600, and as clearing trees in the colonies was a farming prerequisite while its planks could become a consumer product, almost all construction utilized this "free" material. The colonies, particularly Maine, were indeed shipping lumber and masts for ships to England as early as the 1640s.

New England's early meetinghouses (1640s–1700), though basically vernacular in design, "were derived naturally from late medieval English village traditions" (from Marian Card Donnelly's admirable book *The New England Meeting Houses of the Seventeenth Century* [Wesleyan University Press, 1968]). Though only one of these anti–parish church meetinghouses of the seventeenth century survives (Old Ship; 48) documents of other early examples sketch generally squarish, oak-framed buildings, roughly forty feet/ 12 m on a side, topped by thatched roof, with pulpit opposite the entry. One of the first, it is reported, had a small cannon on the roof: the Church of England was probably among the suspected enemies. Many of the very early examples, especially in Connecticut, were of logs.

With increased population and wealth, the outgrown early meetinghouse phased into a longitudinal building, eventually of considerable size, but still with entry opposite the sermon-centric pulpit in the long wall. A square bell tower, at times added later, is often found; galleries are universal. Construction was of oak frame, joined by mortise and tenon, local pine clapboards forming the enclosure. It is this period— basically the 1700s—which characterizes most of the delightful meetinghouses seen here. One might not agree with the liturgy or the sermon, but their bright interior setting is conducive to undisturbed contemplation and worship.

When the American Revolution broke out all building activity ceased. Then with liberty and the eventual revival of construction, the "old" meetinghouse plan withered and the long-axis, sanctuary-at-end plan became popular, the meetinghouse, as the saying goes, "becoming a church." The rise of Unitarianism at the expense of the more rigid Congregationalism probably spurred this development.

The early 1800s produced a magnificent series of churches, by now mostly of brick and largely in the new (i.e., post-Revolution) Federal Style. The influence of England's Sir Christopher Wren and James Gibbs, and America's Asher Benjamin with his book *The Country Builder's Assistant* (1797), were of significant importance, especially with sophisticated urban churches. These straightforward churches often attained an elegant simplicity, outside and in, unknown abroad.

Greek Revival churches followed, beginning around 1820 (spurred by the Greek war of independence), with the Gothic Revival sometimes overlapping. But as the noted critic Montgomery Schuyler (1843–1914) put it, "although there are some earlier churches in a style which the designers of them believed to be Gothic, the Gothic revival in the United States may be said to have begun with the erection of Trinity Church in New York in 1846" (quoted from Baedeker's *United States,* 1909 edition). The Gothic Revival, though today vestigial (partly because of expense), remained until recently as probably America's favorite church architecture, although it was named for barbarians and reflected an eight-hundred-year-old building tradition for a creed not universally subscribed to.

Much of the nineteenth and twentieth centuries consisted in "sniffing about for styles in all past periods" (Giedion, *The Eternal Present: The Beginnings of Architecture* [Pantheon, 1957], p. 26). Some examples were/are capable; most were/are unimpressively timid. The Modern Movement, in a post–World War II effort to bring back the vitality and progressiveness that spurred church architecture for centuries (as will be seen later), continues its patient, difficult search. Several first-rate examples are discussed in this book.

It should be mentioned that "up-to-dateness" played a major role in almost all the lovely churches discussed, few of them escaping interior "modernization," at times to the point of desecration. Even Old Ship Meetinghouse, at 1681 our earliest example, underwent ghastly alterations, while 110 years after its completion the congregation voted to tear it down as being dowdy compared to "the new Wren style"! Fortunately execution was stayed. Today, our admirable and growing preservation movement is restoring many of these religious talismans, vastly enriching our heritage.

The dates and building data appearing here came largely from individual church bulletins with backup from the National Register Nomination Forms which were invaluable sources of information, being almost always more extensive than the National Register final listings. The dates given reflect the building's dedication, subsequent changes being noted in the description.

The focus of this guide is an appreciation of the unique houses of worship which New England produced and nourished for over three hundred years. The selection of the one hundred examples which follow—out of 133 personally visited—will understandably lead to questioning as to why this and not that. Weather at times played a role, tastebuds could be idiosyncratic, while weary distances at times might eliminate a candidate. (We drove some 4,000 miles.) It is thought, however, that those discussed here—all are of merit, some are great—would enrich the visitor. In many cases the surrounding cemeteries will also prove fascinating. These houses of worship and the villages whose profiles they so picturesquely punctuate are national treasures. Bon voyage—I hope you enjoy them as much as we did.

For Further Reading

An increasing number of books are being devoted to the charms of New England. Among the recent ones concerned with its religious heritage are *Meeting House and Church in Early New England* by Edmund W. Sinnott (McGraw-Hill, 1963), a highly useful book-guide listing a total of 500 buildings; *New England Churches and Meetinghouses* by Peter T. Mallary with excellent photographs by Tim Imrie (The Vendome Press, 1985); *Great New England Churches* by Robert Mutrux (Globe Pequot Press, 1982)—65 well-documented examples; *New England Meeting House and Church* by Peter Benes and Philip D. Zimmerman (Boston, 1979). For the specialist, J. Frederick Kelly's two-volume *Early Connecticut Meetinghouses* (Columbia University Press, 1948) is a monumental one-state analysis; Marian Card Donnelly's *The New England Meeting Houses of the Seventeenth Century* (Wesleyan University Press, 1968) gives expert insight into a little-known period.

Several books covering religious architecture in the whole United States are also available: *American Churches* by Roger G. Kennedy (Stewart, Tabori & Chang, 1982)—handsomely illustrated and broad; and *The Colonial Houses of Worship in America* by Harold W. Rose (Hastings House, 1963)—wonderfully thorough.

Note on the Photographs

The great majority of the photographs were taken with a 4 × 5″ Swiss Sinar view camera using filmpacks, the others with a cherished Rolleiflex. No artificial lights were used as most interiors were designed to be content with daylight. (Moreover I don't have any.)

ACKNOWLEDGMENTS

Four talented individuals contributed enormously to this book, indeed, made it possible: Wendy J. Strothman, the director of Beacon Press, who rashly asked me to write this guide; my wife, Dorothea, whose architectural acumen honed both building selections and descriptions; Patricia Edwards Clyne, who meticulously edited an oft-prolix manuscript, always to its betterment; and James Parks Morton, the polymathic Dean of the Cathedral Church of St. John the Divine, whose Foreword gives such elegant perspective—on both religion and architecture—to the whole book. Without these four there would have been no book. Thomas Fischer, Pam Pokorney (both of Beacon Press), and Richard Pace handsomely put it all together.

The heavy expenses of travel in all six New England states, plus related photographic costs, were largely met by a generous grant from the Bank of New England. I am eternally grateful to them.

The ministers and staff of all churches and synagogues were universally helpful. Among those who went out of their way to dig up valuable data are the following: In Connecticut, Nancy L. Wallack of the Connecticut Historical Commission; the Rev. Robert S. Hundley, First Church of Christ, Simsbury. In Maine, Earl Shuttleworth, Maine Historical Preservation Commission; Walter Sherman, Wicasset. In Massachusetts, Lorna Condon and the staff of the Society for the Preservation of New England Antiquities; Beatriz M. Quiroga and Anne Tait of the Massachusetts Historical Commission; the Rev. E. Clifford Cutler, St. Stephen's Episcopal Church, Cohasset; Bob Cable, Secretary of Christ Church, Cambridge; Edwin Charles Lynn, Danvers; the Rev. Kim K. Crawford Harvie, Provincetown; Mrs. Dorothy G. Wrigley, United First Parish, Quincy. In New Hampshire, Gail Ford, New Hampshire Division of Historic Resources; Judy Danforth for data on the Francestown Meetinghouse; Nancy Chamberlain, Secretary of South Congregational Church, Newport; Margaret Greenan, Unitarian Universalist Church, Portsmouth. In Rhode Island, Anne Angelone, Rhode Island Historic Preservation Commission; Professor Emeritus William H. Jordy, Brown University; Nancy Smith Russell, Beneficent Congregational Church, Providence. In Vermont, Gina Campoli, Vermont Division for Historic Preservation.

The Beacon Guide to

New England

Houses of Worship

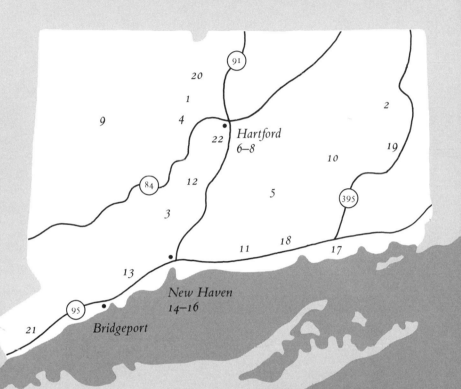

CONNECTICUT

Scale

0 ——————— 10 miles
0 ————— 10 kilometers

91

20

1

9   4

         22   Hartford
              6–8

84   12

         3

                    5

                              10

                                   19

                                        2

                              395

           11   18   17

13

    New Haven
    14–16

95

21   Bridgeport

N

I

CONGREGATIONAL CHURCH
[1819]

6 West Main Street; junction of US
    202 and 44
Avon

David Hoadley, architect

David Hoadley (1774–1839), born in
Waterbury, and his contemporary
Lavius Fillmore (1767–1846), born in
Norwich, were two of Connecticut's
most distinguished architects at the
beginning of the nineteenth century.
Each designed first-rank churches at
the time when earlier "meetinghouses" were phasing out to become
the longitudinal, altar-focused
churches which have characterized
most Christian houses of worship
ever since. The work of both of
these architects is represented in this
book, Fillmore's two finest being in
Vermont (95, 97).

Hoadley's Federal Style Avon
church is notable for its skillful facade and steeple. There is visual
tautness in the projected three-bay
entry with stretched Ionic pilasters, a
smart relationship between fan-lit
doors and windows, and assured
detailing over all. The flush wood
siding and the verticality of the pilasters give prominence to the front by
contrast with the clapboards (4-inch/
10-cm exposure) that encircle the
rest of the building. On the square
tower rises the octagonal belfry (louvers added), topped by an elaborate
lantern with octagonal spire and
weather vane. Balustrades, urns, and
rich treatment attend all. The worship room, which measures 40 feet/
12 m wide by 43 feet/13 m long, is
of basic simplicity with coved ceiling, galleries on three sides (as with
Christopher Wren and James Gibbs
in England), slip pews, and a non-
notable pulpit. As usual the interior
was altered in the mid nineteenth
century when four windows and an
arched opening in the wall behind
the pulpit were closed to make a rear
addition. A fire in 1876 caused both
interior and exterior damage and the
hurricane of 1938 blew off the spire:
all, however, is now in excellent
shape having been most recently refurbished in the 1950s. Though perhaps unremarkable on the interior,
the Avon church is splendid outside.

4

2

OLD TRINITY EPISCOPAL CHURCH
[1771]

Church Street; 2 miles/3.2 km east
of Brooklyn, left off US 6
Brooklyn

Godfrey Malbone, designer

In a well-treed bucolic setting behind a rustic dry-stone wall stands—unexpectedly—a very sophisticated small Georgian church. Its single black round-headed entry and segmental-arched side windows, with three round-headed windows above, set up subtle geometry. A simple pediment and pilasters mark the front door. The church's boxlike form (3-inch/76-mm clapboard exposure) is capped by a hip roof without steeple (like several in Virginia). Trees and tombs picturesquely embrace it. The nave, which measures 30 feet/9.1 m wide by 46 feet/14 m long, is tightly packed with the side balconies pressing the central space. The paneling of pulpit and galleries should be noted. The area around the sanctuary is unusual in that the aisle widens, thus diminishing the pews, so that worshipers can gather around the altar for communion, a change which probably dates from late in the nineteenth century. Otherwise the interior is remarkably as built: it is used today only for celebratory services. Although the church's designer, Colonel Godfrey Malbone, was "but a poor architect," Trinity Episcopal is a very fresh design, particularly in its compact exterior. It is the oldest Episcopal church still standing in Connecticut. (The church should not be confused with the Unitarian Universalist Church in central Brooklyn, which dates from 1772 [restored 1960], nor with the nearby Trinity Parish Church from 1865. Both are also worth a visit.)

3

FIRST CONGREGATIONAL CHURCH
[1827]

Main Street (US 10)
Cheshire

David Hoadley, architect

One of the rewards of the meeting-house in Cheshire lies in its setting: removed from the busy highway with a park and Civil War memorial as frontage, it rises detached from the now bustling town. The church is a worthy partner to its site, both outside and in. The exterior, with its projected porch upheld by four fluted Ionic columns and punctuated by well-turned steeple, can be seen in several other Connecticut churches, those at Litchfield and Milford (9, 13) differing only in detail. The steeple on Hoadley's church at Avon (1) is also very similar to the one here in Cheshire. (Incidentally, the Avon facade virtually duplicates Cheshire's without the projected porch.) All of the four steeples mentioned consist of an octagonal belfry (at times louvered) on the first stage, balustraded and urned second stage, or lantern, often fancy, with octagonal or round spire on top, and weather vane twirling above. Only the rectangular window in the pediment is ill at ease.

The interior of the Cheshire church, which measures 50 feet/15 m by 58 feet/17.7 m, is straightforward, even demure, focusing on the pulpit with its double stair and discreet (modern) Palladian framing. The ceiling is bowed in a large ovoid dome (note the edge decoration) from which a prominent chandelier (1968) is suspended. In 1857, following severe damage by storm, a number of changes were made in the interior—including elaborate stenciling—and they continued to be made until respectful restoration in 1968. The detailing throughout is excellent.

Although David Hoadley is not specifically recorded as the architect of the church, the noted J. Frederick Kelly in his two-volume *Early Connecticut Meetinghouses* (Columbia University Press, 1948) writes, "So fine a design leaves us no choice but to believe that it is the work of an architect of no mean ability . . . it seems but logical to regard Hoadley . . . as its author." So does the National Register Nomination Form of 1975.

FIRST CHURCH OF CHRIST,
CONGREGATIONAL [1772]

Main Street (CT 10) at Church
Farmington

*Captain Judah Woodruff, designer-
builder*

The village of Farmington, founded
in the 1640s, is one of Connecticut's
most delightful. Its substantial
houses (generally white) are meticulously maintained, their contiguous
lawns well cut, the commercial area
unobtrusive. It also boasts the First
Church of Christ, Congregational,
one of New England's finest and the
third of its faith. In shape the church
is a gabled oblong box, 74 feet/
22.5 m wide by 50/15.2 m deep,
with the main entrance on the long
side. (There is also a small entry
porch on the south side). A square
tower, octagonal belfry, and spire
are attached to the north end. It con-
stitutes a climax to that stage of
meetinghouse evolution, whereby
the entry is in the middle of the long
(street) side directly opposite the pulpit. By 1800 most plans had the entry at the narrow end, the altar
longitudinally at the far end, with

the result that, as has often been said, the meetinghouse became a church. (The Virginia brick churches of this time, representing the Church of England, were always of this long-axis plan.) The Farmington meetinghouse/church, almost domestically proportioned, rises to distinction in its famous spire atop its very tall tower. Its open octagonal belfry, neatly balustraded, supports the modest lantern stage, while above with elegant fairing rises the 150-foot/45.7-m high spire. Reputedly it was built in telescoping sections on the ground and raised in place! The Greek Revival entry portico in the middle of the long side was added in 1834 along with the blinds, both accents to the good. The clapboards, almost all original, have an unusually narrow exposure (2½ to 3½ inches/63–88.9 mm, fastened with handmade nails. (Incidentally, it was the machine production of nails and the mill output of handy one-man two-by-fours in the 1830s and '40s which revolutionized building in this country.)

The interior of First Church embraces light while its wide, stepped galleries on three sides develop unusually close intimacy with the pulpit. The pulpit, deacon's seat, and organ housing were completely restored in 1952, having been alarmingly mishandled in the last century. A Farmington native, Captain Judah Woodruff, was the designer-builder.

5

FIRST CHURCH OF CHRIST,
CONGREGATIONAL [1794]

Off CT 151 via CT 82 east of East
  Haddam
East Haddam

Lavius Fillmore, probable architect

An unexpectedly accomplished church far removed from town and river set amidst a private domain of trees and a cemetery. Although the mass of the church is straightforward, indeed routine, except for the round-headed windows on the second floor, the stages of the steeple are fresh and expert. The square tower repeats on three sides the round-headed windows of those below, but here they are heavily framed and surmounted by a cornice with thick balustrade on top. The belfry is set back and forms another square with double pilasters and prominent cornice. A sharp, angular spire (rebuilt) rises above. There is almost a campanile quality to this tower.

The interior, which measures approximately 47 feet/14.3 m wide by 52 feet/15.8 m long, is full of light and air from its tall round-headed upper windows. A shallow dome hovers over all, the pulpit wall is chaste, altogether "one of the finest in the state" (J. Frederick Kelly, *Early Connecticut Meetinghouses* 1948). Lavius Fillmore, whose two Vermont churches (95, 97) are superb, is generally thought to have been the designer and builder of this gem at East Haddam.

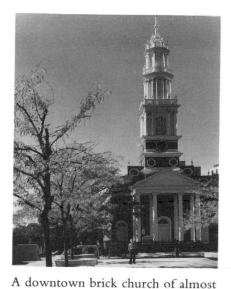

FIRST CHURCH OF CHRIST [1807]

Main Street at Gold
Hartford

Daniel Wadsworth, designer

A downtown brick church of almost unprecedented richness for its date at the beginning of the nineteenth century. That it had no trained architect as designer—Wadsworth was simply a prominent citizen—makes the result doubly impressive. An amalgam of influences from London must have helped Wadsworth, for elements from several of Christopher Wren's fifty-two churches—plus the work of James Gibbs—can be seen. (The belfry stage resembles Wren's St. Stephen, Walbrook, 1679, for instance.) Whatever the inspiration, the results are capable, though nudging the ambitious. Note that the tower sports an "extra" cornice at midheight while the belfry above not only luxuriates in a rich broken entablature but boasts tracery in its louvers. The third stage clusters sixteen Ionic columns around its octagonal drum, all protected by a prominent balustrade. The slightly smaller fourth stage has only eight columns with, above, a small drum and a metal finial. Total height is 185 feet/ 56.4 m. Decorative panels give accent to the facade. The three entry doors each open onto a separate vestibule.

The oft-altered audience room is notable for the two-story-high Ionic columns, three per side, which support the lateral balconies and give verticality to the space, which measures 60 feet/18.2 m square, excluding sanctuary. The original nave ceiling was flat with flat coffered ceilings over the galleries (which were lowered in 1835); in 1852 the central portion was vaulted and the pulpit was set in a recess for greater identity. A fire in 1844 caused severe damage so that "no original work now remains."

The Ancient Burying Ground, which lies adjacent, has stones from the 1660s; it is still owned by the City of Hartford.

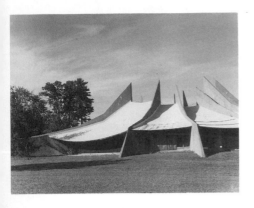

UNITARIAN MEETINGHOUSE
[1964]

50 Bloomfield Avenue, off US 44 at
    CT 189
Hartford

Victor A. Lundy, architect

Looking like a biblical tent whose twelve supports scratch the sky, this Unitarian church in a quiet field of suburban West Hartford promises refuge with excitement. There is a gathering-of-the-faithful quality about the exterior with its angled concrete fins focused on the infinite. (Incidentally, the use of twelve supports had nothing to do with tribes or disciples: it resulted as an economy from the fifteen initially planned. Note that they vary in both height and spacing.) Inside this geometric centricity one encounters a gigantic inverted cornucopia of thin wood strips bowed gracefully upward and hovering over the entire congregation. Supported by steel cables attached to the radial walls, the outreach of this protective wooden tent binds worshipers together in unity, while over the sanctuary the centric focus of the wooden strips disappears heavenward. No religious symbolism is used. Church school, offices, and services surround the worship room with Plexiglas divisions separating them. Problems exist—transmitted noise is noticeable—but this is a very imaginative church. As the brochure mentions, quoting the architect, it can well be "a symbolic and lyrical interpretation of the Unitarian faith."

THE CATHEDRAL OF ST. JOSEPH
[1962]

140 Farmington Avenue
Hartford

Eggers & Higgins, architects

The commanding mass of this extraordinary Roman Catholic cathedral is based on a sturdy U-shaped form, its geometry relieved by vertical piers and a tapered tower which rises 306 feet/93 m to the top of its cross. (The tower recalls that by Auguste Perret, 1874–1954, the pioneering French architect, for his post-war church at Le Havre; it, too, is called St. Joseph.) The sculpted frieze of the entry depicts St. Joseph, his cloak upheld by angels. Its travertine was sculpted by Tommaso Peccini. The bronze doors are by Enzo Assenza.

The formalistic limestone exterior gives no hint of the breath-taking interior: here, indeed, is the inspiration of Paris's famous Sainte Chapelle (A.D. 1247) advancing, like the probing development of Gothic architecture, to erupt into the late twentieth century: color and luminosity for our time. It is useful to note that the windows in the Sainte Chapelle, which is also U-shaped in plan, measure 13 feet/4 m wide by 49 feet/14.9 m high; those in St. Joseph are

13½ feet/4.1 m wide by 67 feet/20.4 m high. In each church the glass completely fills the space between the frames, in St. Joseph a frame of reinforced concrete. The glass here is not the thin medieval variety but *Betonglas* or slab glass made of 3/4–1 inch/19–25 mm thick pieces set in cement, a technique largely developed by Gabriel Loire of Chartres who was responsible for the exciting glass in Wallace Harrison's First Presbyterian Church in Stamford, Connecticut (21). The twenty-six Hartford windows were designed by Jean Barillet of Paris under the overall art direction of the International Institute of Liturgical Art in Rome. (A guide folder to the glass and the church is available.) The faceted quality of *Betonglas* responds to the movement of the sun over its surfaces, thus giving the windows an alive quality as the sun moves through the heavens. The overall theme of the moderately abstracted windows is "Saviour in the Gospels." The nave, 153 feet/46.6 m long by 108 feet/32.9 m high, and seating 1,750, is enveloped by glass except for part of the narthex end and the panel behind the sanctuary. The ceiling is of flat aluminum panels with downlights furnishing illumination.

The 80-foot/24.4 m high, 40-foot/12.2-m wide ceramic tile reredos, representing "The Saviour in Glory," was designed by Enzo Assenza. A simple marble altar stands in front with an arresting 44-foot/13.4-m high aluminum baldachino above. Designed by the architects and sculpted by Gleb Derujinsky, it forms a tripod—the Trinity—with its legs crowned by archangels, the finial topped by the archangel Michael. Brilliant. The Bishop's Throne—the *cathedra*—at left is of walnut. Six small ambulatory chapels open off the sanctuary; in addition there are one-story congregational chapels branching on either side of the nave. A Lower Church seats 1,330. The original cathedral, finished in 1892, burned in 1956.

9

FIRST CONGREGATIONAL
CHURCH [1829]

The Green, US 202 at Torrington
    Road
Litchfield

The village of Litchfield, founded in
1719, has become increasingly popular in recent years, partly due to its
notable architectural inheritance, but
also because its 1,100-foot/335-m el-
evation promises finer air while early
on it discouraged industrial development. As the National Register of
Historic Places put it, Litchfield is an
"excellent example of a typical 18th
C. New England town." The anchor
of its architectural attractions (most
of which are private but visible from
the road) is this handsome meetinghouse: few have had a stranger history. The first meetinghouse (1724)
was a primitive shelter used for religious and town meetings (and for
storing gunpowder for defense
against Indians). In 1761 the second
church was built reflecting the
growth of the village and prevalent
architectural styles. (Old South in
Boston was of influence.) In 1829
this, the third church, was constructed, both larger and more impressive than its predecessor. Less
than a half-century later, the minister
and congregation, falling under the
modish spell of Victorian Gothic—
Ruskin again—decided that such
simple "Colonial" architecture was

old-fashioned and had no "taste or beauty" (Henry Ward Beecher). But instead of dismantling the old or third church, they simply moved it up Torrington Road, where it served as a meeting hall and eventually as a movie house shorn of spire. A proper wooden "Gothic" church was then erected (1873) on the site. However, in the early twentieth century the opinion began to be expressed that a "medieval" church on a New England village green of Colonial background was an anachronism. Sentiment grew for a return of the still-standing third church, and in 1929–30 the fourth or Gothic church was torn down. Thereupon the third church was moved back to its old site and thoroughly rehabilitated! Richard H. Dana was the restoration architect.

The exterior of the present (and third) church has close resemblance to several others in Connecticut, notably Cheshire and Milford by David Hoadley (3, 13), but no reference to an architect has been found. The church's asymmetric relation to the Common and its command of the uphill road give it great urban presence. Its projected portico adds to its stateliness while tower, belfry, lantern, and spire poke knowingly into the sky. The audience room, which measures approximately 50 feet/15 m wide and 64 feet/20 m long, is of straightforward simplicity with almost suppressed balconies quietly bordering the nave, a slight dome filling the ceiling, and a superb pulpit with graceful twin stairs dominating the sanctuary. Only the two windows high in the end wall distract. Altogether one of the most rewarding.

FIRST CONGREGATIONAL CHURCH [1807]

South edge of Lebanon Green
Lebanon

Colonel John Trumbull, designer

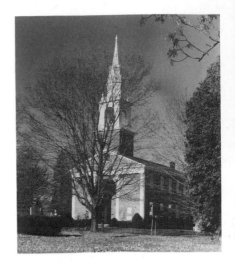

First Congregational is one of New England's most original early nineteenth-century churches in one of its most pleasant towns. The church's compact brick form, inset ellipsoidal entry, and well-handled steeple give it a unique personality. The entry is monumentalized by four white half-columns which flank it and by the denticulated entablature and pediment above. (The main door does not live up to this splendor.) The brick tower with three properly scaled clocks is topped by a square open belfry with two octagonal stages above supporting spire and gilded weather vane. All of this wood superstructure was hurled through the roof and onto the nave by the infamous hurricane of 1938, destroying not only the roof but most of the church except for the front portion. Complete reconstruction was undertaken by J. Frederick Kelly, a renowned expert, who carefully took the church back to its original Trumbull design. (Earlier "improvements," including the insertion of a second floor in 1875, had left the worship room "totally devoid of interest.") Delayed by World War II, rebuilding was not completed until 1954. The restored compact nave (40 feet/12 m by 52 feet/16 m) is notable for its detailing, especially in the panels of the galleries which have square supports below and round ones above. The Palladian window behind the pulpit seems overscaled for the size of its wall but it is as designed, as can be seen in the original brickwork outside. John Trumbull, son of Governor Jonathan Trumbull, Sr., was one of the greatest artists of the Revolutionary period; this is his only building. It is highly likely that during his studies in London he was impressed by Christopher Wren's churches there.

The irregular stretch of the Lebanon Green behind the church should be noted.

II

FIRST CONGREGATIONAL
CHURCH [1838]

20 Meetinghouse Lane
Madison

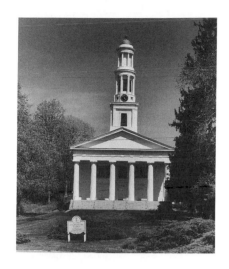

Facing a spacious, unstructured common framed by polite and often historic houses, First Congregational's setting is one of comfortable peace. In this untroubled bower rests a very white, very pure example of the Greek Revival at its liturgical best. The gabled body of the church is canonical as regards Hellenic proportion and meticulousness of detail. Above—mirroring the height of the church itself from stylobate to peak of pediment—rises the steeple, with square, paneled belfry, round becolumned lantern on hexagonal base, round upper stage, and low gilded dome. The interior carries out the simplicity of the exterior including its Greek Revival inspiration. The centric elevated pulpit stands in front of an unusual alcove, powerfully framed by double pilasters, with two inset Doric columns and a gilded cross in the center. Pulpit and setting are carefully detailed. The galleries on three sides are supported by slender fluted Doric columns. Downlights augment the chandeliers.

As so often happened in the mid nineteenth century, the church was substantially altered (1867), being lengthened to 56 feet/17 m wide by 76 feet/23.1 m long, its ceiling modified from domical to flat, and *trompe l'oeil* frescoes added. In 1956 the alcove was rebuilt and most of the fool-the-eye painting eliminated. The architect of this well-bred church is not known.

CENTER CONGREGATIONAL
CHURCH [1830]

Broad and East Main streets
Meriden

Sidney M. Stone, architect

The entire facade of Center Church—like that in Madison of 1838 (11)—is a Greek temple whose six stalwart Doric columns hold down its important corner location. A superior steeple rises directly behind. The church is one of the examples of the Greek Revival period of architecture which, following the "Colonial," influenced much American architecture from Philadelphia (Second Bank of the United States, 1824) to Louisiana's verandahed plantations. The Colonial period had indeed employed Classic elements (porticos, entablatures, columns, etc.), but the Greek Revival went far beyond and imitated a proper Hellenic temple. The style reflects that era when the "romance" of Greece's War of Independence (1820–21), fueled by Byron's passionate writing, sprouted architectural sympathy. Whether this "pagan" style was appropriate for a Christian church is moot, but in Meriden (as in Madison) we find one of its most faithful religious examples.

Behind the accurately proportioned wood columns of the front are three prominently detailed identical doorways framed by pilasters and topped by a full entablature. The steeple is of four stages: modest square base with clock, louvered belfry with Doric pilasters, octagonal louvered lantern with Ionic details, and circular drum with dome, all capably profiled. The interior of the church (48 feet/14.6 m by 55 feet/16.7 m) has been so altered that little remains of the original. In 1872 the west end was extended 20 feet/6 m for pulpit and organ recess. Sidney M. Stone's name is given as probable architect; he had studied with Ithiel Town, whose influence can be seen here.

Adjacent to Center Church (which is not to be confused with Meriden's downtown First Congregational Church of the 1870s) stands the First Baptist Church of 1786, handsome in its own right.

13

FIRST UNITED CHURCH OF CHRIST [1824]

West Main and West River streets
Milford

David Hoadley, architect

Milford, just south of Interstate 95, is one of Connecticut's earliest settlements, dating from 1639. Among its landmarks is First United, thought to be one of several similar churches designed by David Hoadley. This example overlooks the slope of the Town Green though regrettably cut off from it by roads. Like Hoadley's 1827 church at Cheshire (3), as well as the 1829 unattributed Congregational Church at Litchfield (9), the Milford fane has a prominent portico whose four Ionic columns uphold entablature and pediment. Above and rising as a pharos for the faithful are tower, louvered octagonal belfry, lantern, and spire, all delicately detailed. It should be mentioned that Hoadley's Avon Church (1), finished in 1819, has a tower steeple much like this.

The dignified interior of the Milford church, soberly white and light gray, and measuring 52 feet/15.8 m wide by 67 feet/20.4 m long, conforms to the normal pattern of five windows per side, slightly domed ceiling, galleries on three sides, raised pulpit, and prominent organ. In 1868, 15 feet/4.6 m were added to the worship room and the whole building repaired. Minor changes, including frescoes, were carried out through the years, when in 1918 the whole worship room was reversed and the chancel moved to its present location. In 1939 the interior was redecorated by the noted J. Frederick Kelly.

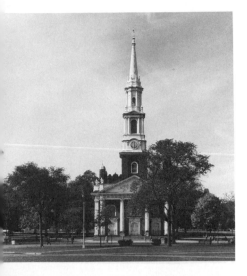

14

Temple Street between Elm and
  Chapel
New Haven

Ithiel Town, architect

The New Haven Green is unique in
Colonial town planning for its early
date and for its size. Measuring 825
feet/251 m on a side (supposedly 500
Old Testament cubits) it was platted
in 1638 as the center of nine equally
dimensioned squares and served as
market place for the fast-growing
town. It is quite likely that the overall basic dimensions and mathematical layout had been determined
before New Haven's first settlers
arrived from Massachusetts as little
advantage was taken of the nearby
harbor. The Green is still the graceful heart of the city (now 126,000)
and an urban delight.

The Green is also unique in having
three churches side by side, all built
within two years of each other
(1814–16). That one of them numbers among the earliest examples of
the Gothic Revival and the other
two—both stylistically similar—reflect the Federal, dramatically under-
lines the vagaries and fashions of
religious architecture in this country.
(Vagaries and fashions still obtain.)

The First Church of Christ, more
familiarly Center Church, has one of
the most magnificent facades of any
church in this country. Its slightly
projected portico carries a rich "Roman" entablature, while the tympa-

num in the pediment above rejoices in an almost baroque series of carved wood swags. Note also the grandeur of the three doors. Above rises a square brick tower, its round-headed windows set in recessed arches reflecting those in the entry and sides. A clock stage, its cornice cleverly arched (Gibbs's influence), is topped by a square louvered belfry with half-round head; above, an octagonal lantern, rich with broken entablature, dances with urns. Capping all this is a conical spire 192 feet/59 m in height. The two sides of the church are marked in the Federal fashion by recessed arched panels in its brick walls, with round-headed windows above and arced windows below. A vigorous parapet with urns crowns each side.

Today's cheerful interior, measuring 68 feet/21 m wide by 75 feet/ 23 m long, was substantially changed in 1842–43 to "the newest fashion" under the direction of Henry Austin. Chancel windows were walled up, the pulpit changed, frescoes adorned walls and ceiling, and drab paint applied to interior woodwork and exterior brick. (Austin, an accomplished architect, should have known better.) In 1912 the exterior paint was sandblasted off and in 1959–60 the entire interior was taken back to its original, early nineteenth-century condition. The spacious auditorium is now dominated by a memorial window—the Davenport Window (1894)—set in a broad frame with raised platform for clergy beneath. The window was designed by Joseph Lauber of the Tiffany Studio and depicts Davenport, "the spiritual architect of the New Haven Colony," preaching the congregation's first sermon in 1638. Ten other stained glass windows were also installed in the 1890s. The lightly domed ceiling carries a crystal chandelier (contemporary). There is an unusual crypt beneath the church containing 135 graves.

The National Register of Historic Places says that the church was "built from a Federal design initiated by Asher Benjamin and completed by Ithiel Town." Town later merged talents with Alexander Jackson Davis, the firm of Town & Davis subsequently becoming noted for its Greek Revival work. James Gibbs's St. Martin-in-the-Fields Church in London (1715) is generally cited as being of inspiration, particularly in the tower, but this church rises to heights on its own.

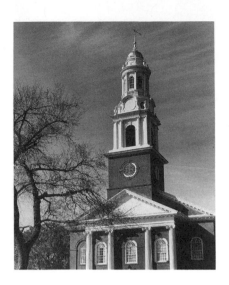

15

THE UNITED CHURCH [1815]

The Green
New Haven

David Hoadley, architect

A patrician Federal Style brick
church which occupies its corner site
with dignity. The projected front, its
pediment supported by four Ionic
engaged columns, frames three
round-headed doors—The Trinity—
and an equal number of round-
headed windows, with the circle
motif being repeated above. The
doors are identical in size but the
central entry is made prominent by
doubled half-columns with entablature. Note the wider bay of the center. The tower is outstanding in its
upward projection from the church
and in the compactly knit stages
above. The square brick base, with
abstracted "world" on three sides
(the global mission of the church),
supports a robust belfry, its openings
edged by both Ionic columns and pilasters. The stages above show great
imagination: the intermediate level
has a broken circular cornice, followed by an elegant round lantern

with urns and swags, then a gilded dome. Note that the half-dome rests on small globes. (As several references point out, there is an influence here of James Gibbs's work and book in England.) The architect of United Church reputedly did not want his tower to compete with neighboring Center Church's 192-foot/59-m spire. The result he achieved is masterful, one of New England's finest. Incidentally, the handling of the rear facades of both churches should be noted. United's measurements are approximately 68 feet/21 m wide by 96 feet/29 m long.

The bright interior of the United Church—like most of those dating from the early nineteenth century—has been often changed to be in "the modern style." As early as 1842 the large window in the wall (then flat) behind the pulpit was bricked in—one source mentions five windows—and eight years later the arched recess for the pulpit was created and the galleries lowered. (The interiors of Center Church and United are very similar except for pulpit wall.) Shortly thereafter the entire church, outside and in, was painted white—including the brickwork. The exterior was sandblasted back to natural brick in 1937, and in 1967, for the church's 225th anniversary, complete renovation, including the present pulpit, took place.

Though some sources mention Ebenezer Johnson, Jr., as architect, J. Frederick Kelly (in *Early Connecticut Meetinghouses*) dismisses Johnson as a "contractor" and maintains that "not only should the design be attributed to Hoadley in its entirety, but we must also regard it as his masterpiece." Edmund W. Sinnott in his *Meetinghouse and Church in Early New England* (McGraw-Hill, 1963) also credits the church to Hoadley.

16

TRINITY EPISCOPAL CHURCH
[1816]

The Green
New Haven

Ithiel Town, architect

The ambidextrous Ithiel Town, while working on Center Church next door, was also producing drawings for Trinity. Center Church (14) is Federal in its inspiration and has perhaps threescore cousins throughout the state; Trinity, on the other hand, is Gothic Revival, one of the earliest of that style in this country, and consequently of considerable influence in making this style popular. It measures 74 feet/23 m wide by 103 feet/31 m long. Unfortunately the restrained, even subdued exterior of Trinity which we see today is not what it was during most of the last century. Initially its tower, then taller, almost bristled with pinnacles, while finials ran around all roof edges. However, unlike the stone walls of the church, these ornaments were made of wood, and weather took its toll; in 1870 the tower was made masonry to its peak, topped by a red slate pyramidal roof (removed in 1930), and the finials were taken off.

The interior of Trinity, though oft-changed, shines with "uncommon grandeur" (Kelly) via a parade of gilt-tinged arches marching down the nave. These are upheld by typically clustered stone piers (originally of wood) bridged by broad gallery facing. Henry Austin, the well-known New Haven architect, redecorated the interior and its frescoes in 1847—as he did Center Church adjacent. In 1885 the chancel was extended 25 feet/7.6 m, making the church more "Gothic," hence—purposefully—"less like its neighbors," and in 1906 the interior was redecorated. The present reredos dates from 1912. A complete renovation of the interior took place in 1961–62. Though not as was, Trinity still rewards as is.

ST. JAMES [1850]

Huntington and Federal Streets
New London

Richard Upjohn, architect

Richard Upjohn (1802–78) was one of the most distinguished architects of the last century. Born in England and trained as a cabinetmaker, he emigrated with his family to Massachusetts (1829) and early worked with Alexander Parris in Boston. He subsequently branched out on his own, eventually achieving enormous fame with his design for Trinity Church (1846) in New York City. Upjohn's many later churches can be seen from Maine and Rhode Island (25, 83) to Texas, almost all in the Gothic Revival style and almost all Episcopal. Upjohn himself was firmly Church of England. Though occasionally working in wood (First Parish in Brunswick, Maine), he is primarily known for the brown New Jersey freestone he employed for the body of numerous churches as well as for tower, belfry, and spire as here in St. James. (See also his Grace Church, Providence, R.I.) St. James, it should be noted, rises abruptly from its frontage on Huntington Street because of grade fall-off.

The church's interior displays the elaborate trusswork frequently seen in Upjohn churches, here marked by a series of cusped arches. Seven stained-glass windows by Louis Comfort Tiffany adorn the nave. Changes were made in the interior through the years, the choir being moved from balcony to chancel (1914), while a complete restoration was undertaken in 1976.

The exterior of St. James is drolly accented by the adjacent lineup of four identical Greek Revival houses—Whale Oil Row—built for local shipping magnates in the 1830s and '40s. The Gothic-Greek architectural counterpoint has never been more divertingly expressed.

FIRST CONGREGATIONAL
CHURCH [1817/1910]

Lyme Street at Ferry Road
Old Lyme

The informally laid out town of
Old Lyme (settled in 1648) with its
meandering main street and set-back
buildings is one of New England's
most appealing, and among its
amenities is this church, strategically
placed at the elbow bend of the
road. The church obviously has architectural cousins around the state
but there is more sophistication here,
particularly in the steeple, than seen
elsewhere. Unfortunately the church
which was originally built on this
site burned to the ground in 1907.
Its replacement is, however, as exact
a copy as could be made at the time,
and will reward the visitor both outside and in. The old foundations,
measuring 49'2"/15 m by 58'6"/
18 m were of great help in the reconstruction. Ernest S. Greene, a
well-known church architect in the
earlier years of this century, was in
charge of rebuilding and used, of
course, as much fireproof material as
possible.

The projected front is seen in several of David Hoadley's churches (including those at Cheshire and Milford; 3, 13), but Old Lyme Congregational has finer proportions. Its steeple is very superior. Note that the half-round heads of the three front doors are echoed slightly in the almost tiny half-round in the pediment and are dramatically stated in the full circle of the three black clocks in the tower and echoed above. The tower itself projects only modestly above the ridge, unlike the awkward extensions often seen. Above the tower a square, not octagonal, stage houses the belfry with four louvered openings. The lantern stage is octagonal, its eight smaller openings topped by a balustrade with urns. An octagonal spire punctuates all at 139 feet/42 m. It is the articulated quality of these elements and the progressive diminution of the circle/half-circle which make this tower so successful.

The bright interior is focused on a wide exedra or arched niche for the raised pulpit. Its gold-painted acanthus band is also seen in the slightly domed ceiling. The original interior was remodeled in 1850 and the apse (with undistinguished railing) was added in 1886. The upper and lower windows on both sides can be shielded by inside shutters. Samuel Belcher was the church's builder but its talented architect is not known.

The Village of Old Lyme is under Historic District preservation, while the lovely outlying wetlands by the Connecticut River are very much the concern of the Old Lyme Conservation Trust. May all efforts be successful.

19

CONGREGATIONAL CHURCH
[1816]

Main Street (CT 12)
Plainfield

Ithiel Town, architect

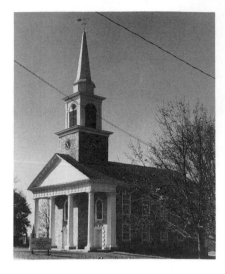

A little-known but sturdy small church (47 feet/14.3 m by 70 feet/21.3 m overall). The combination of warm-colored ashlar gneiss and the precisely detailed, white-painted wood portico, the whole topped by square stone tower, belfry, and spire (of wood and not original), make a well-knit whole. (The side walls and rear of the church are laid in random ashlar.) The smooth-faced pediment, it should be noted, is an extension of the gabled roof. The three identical entries, boldly rusticated in the English, James Gibbs fashion (via Gibbs's study in Italy in the early 1700s), seem small under the tall arced windows but the overall effect is very fresh.

In 1850–51 the church was divided into two floors with audience room on upper level and social activities on ground floor. Subsequently other changes were carried out with the result that no original (i.e., Ithiel Town) interior work remains. Regrettable. Restoration is now in progress. Incidentally, the church was built in stone—unusual for its time—because the 1784 meeting-house of wood had been flattened by a hurricane in 1815. Ithiel Town (1784–1844), it will be remembered, was also the architect for two of the churches on New Haven's Green (14, 15). And as a qualified engineer—possibly the finest of his time—he designed and patented the Town Truss for bridges, the royalties from which helped support him financially. The church was also used for town meetings until 1872 when the Town Hall was built.

20

FIRST CHURCH OF CHRIST [1830]

Off US 202, south edge of town
Simsbury

Damon & Hayden, designer-builders

The Simsbury church occupies a detached site set back from the highway. Its design is unusual in the rectangularity of its square-headed doors and windows and the squareness of each of the three stages of its steeple. The only curved forms are decorative plaques. This angularity might be ascribed to primitiveness but Isaac Damon (1763–1862), who was undoubtedly the designer in the firm of Damon & Hayden—having almost a dozen churches in Massachusetts to his credit—knew exactly what he was doing. Moreover, the profile of the church front and its tower is very accomplished and it commands its site with conviction.

The squared upper windows of the front were given arched tops in the last century but were returned to their proper flat-headed condition following a fire in 1965 which destroyed much of the church. (See church bulletin and J. Frederick Kelly's *Early Connecticut Meetinghouses*.) The interior (50 feet/15 m by 52 feet/16 m), too, was changed following the fire—one of its many alterations—so that little of the original worship room is left. It is now chaste but perhaps overactive at the pulpit end.

The reader may be interested to note that next to the shopping center in town on US 202 stands a full-sized replica of the church's First Meetinghouse of 1683. Constructed in 1970 for Simsbury's Tercentenary, it reproduces as accurately as possible one of the state's—and the Colonies'—earliest if conjectural meetinghouses and is well worth seeing.

21

FIRST PRESBYTERIAN CHURCH
[1958]

1101 Bedford Street off Hoyt
Stamford

Wallace K. Harrison, architect

First Presbyterian is one of the great churches of our time: moreover, it stands for that tradition of nontradition which marked those distinct and glorious steps of Christian architecture from Early Christian and the Byzantine, to the Romanesque, the Gothic, the Renaissance, the Baroque, and the Colonial, each of which searched for architectural answers reflective of its own ethos and each of which was unabashedly "modern" for its time. On approaching the church the free-standing 260-foot/79-m high Carillon Tower (1967) with fifty-six bells sets an angular note that recalls the faceted planes of the exterior of the nave. Angled for added strength, the walls set an intriguing rhythm of slate, concrete, and glass. A sharp bend in the ridge profile marks narthex to right and nave to left: amidst this vigor the entry—in spite of effort—seems almost secretive. The plan of the 720-seat church suggests the shape of a fish, the ancient Christian symbol. It measures 234 feet/71 m long.

If the exterior of First Presbyterian presents an unusual, even puzzling, appearance, when one enters the nave a whole new world—a world of fascinating, mercurial colors—materializes. The nave, which seats 670, is indeed one of our inspired religious spaces. The glass, which appears smooth and unexciting outside, is faceted within and as one proceeds up the aisle, particularly on a bright day, the sun makes a private spotlight of each of the 22,000 1-inch/25 mm-thick prisms. This *Betonglas* (concrete glass), which the French invented and named, is set in panels of concrete, here numbering 152, and can have an almost infinite range of colors. The panels are tied into the structure, hence have a supportive role: "skin" and skeleton meld; there are no columns. As can be seen, the panels extend from floor to ridge (60 feet/18 m). Gabriel Loire, the famous French glassmaster from Chartres, worked closely with Harrison in their design and production. The panels, though abstract, carry symbolism: the Crucifixion on the north (right) side, the Resurrection on south. (A church folder explaining these is available.)

There are a few questionable details, outside and in, concerning the design of First Presbyterian; moreover, the plan is too attenuated for liturgical intimacy, but what a church! The adjacent Sunday school, chapel, fellowship hall, and offices were designed by Sherwood, Smith & Mills.

22

FIRST CHURCH OF CHRIST [1764]

Main and Marsh streets
Wethersfield

Wethersfield was one of the first settlements in Connecticut (1634), its earliest inhabitants arriving from Massachusetts down what is now called the Connecticut River. It is the oldest permanent English community in the state. (New Haven was founded three years later.) The town is noted for its historic district and architectural heritage which its late twentieth-century inhabitants have carefully preserved, with the result that Wethersfield offers unusual amenity.

The First Church of Christ, the third near this site, traces its Congregational background to the early seventeenth century and its Puritan background. Like the three other still-standing Colonial meetinghouses in Connecticut, this at Wethersfield also served for town meetings (until 1838). It is the only one of brick—note the patterning, including quoins, in the brickwork. Although the tower seems powerful for the gabled mass of the church, the wood superstructure of square

belfry, square lantern, and octagonal spire are excellent. It is pertinent to note that the entire steeple was closely, very closely, modeled on that of Christ Church (Old North) in Boston (1724; 36) and in turn found favor in Trinity Church, Newport (1726; 84). The exterior should also be seen from the cemetery at rear.

The worship room, which measures 75 feet/23 m wide by 48 feet/15 m deep, is typical of the mid eighteenth century with raised pulpit and sounding board in the middle of the long wall facing the entry. This chaste interior was several times altered, the most serious attack being in 1882 when it was gothicized in "incredible bad taste" (J. Frederick Kelly, *Early Connecticut Meetinghouses*). Windows were lengthened, second-rate stained glass installed, the floor pitched, and drab paint smeared over all, including the exterior. However, the congregation, which forms one of the largest Congregational churches in New England, realized this desecration, and from 1971 to 1973 completely restored the church to its original condition, basing all work on scholarly research. The interior is now delightful.

34

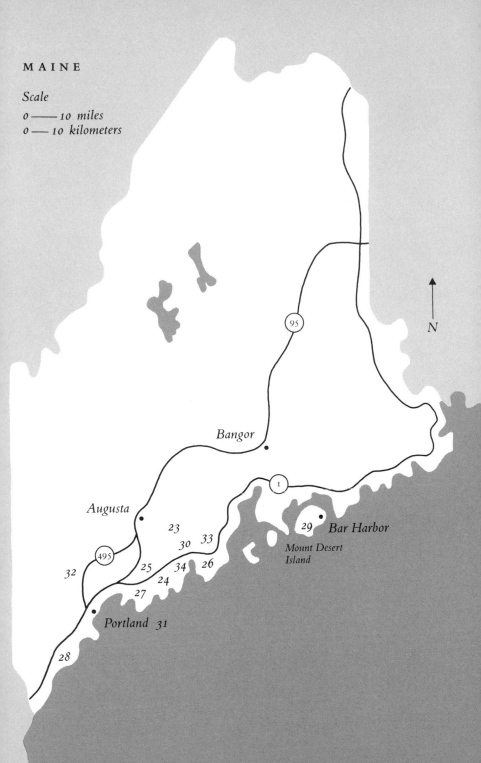

MAINE

Scale
0 ——— 10 miles
0 ——— 10 kilometers

95

Bangor

1

Augusta

23

30   33

29   Bar Harbor

495

Mount Desert
Island

32

25   34   26

24

27

28

Portland 31

N

23

MEETINGHOUSE [1789]

ME 218 (about 7 miles/11 km north
of Wiscasset)
Near Alna

Crowning, in loneliness, a wind-swept hill, the Alna Meetinghouse epitomizes the rigorous demands of Congregational religion in earlier years. Albeit exposed to the elements, it offers a surprising—and sturdy—refuge within; indeed, the progress from the unprotected and plain to comfort and the Word (i.e., pulpit) reflect this. For though the exterior is relatively routine, except for its bright yellow paint and green shutters, the interior is surprisingly accomplished. The pulpit with its sounding board is outstanding, one of the finest with its articulated paneling and color. The spindle-top box pews (5 feet/1.5 m square) and the sculpted columns are also note-worthy. The staircase to the usual three-sided gallery is contained in the projected entrance pavilion. There is, incidentally, only one door. The Meetinghouse was restored by the Pemaquid Chapter of the Daughters of the American Revolution and is now well maintained by the town-ship. The interior can be glimpsed through the windows. The overall measurements are approximately 51 feet/16 m wide by 41 feet/12 m deep.

24

WINTER STREET CHURCH [1844]

Washington Street at Winter
Bath

Anthony C. Raymond, masterbuilder

The exterior of the Winter Street
Church is one of the most imaginative—indeed exuberant—examples
of vernacular Gothic Revival to be
seen. Its twin entrances are set in
ogee arches and flank central lancet-
arch windows, all framed by pilasters and topped by balustrades. The
sturdy tower, with pointed arch
windows like those below, rises
above, the open belfry with its own
arches lightens the mass, while two
more stages top all. The spire is 100
feet/30 m high. Ambitious pinnacles
leap from every corner. Its flush siding is painted white. The setting for
the church, which rises from Washington Street to face a spacious park,
is also rewarding.

The church, however, has been
decommissioned; its interior, which
measures 60 feet/18 m wide by 78
feet/24 m long, needs considerable
attention, and its future is in doubt.
One can only hope that its National
Register status will preserve it and
encourage adaptive usage. To this
end local citizens have created the
Sagadahoc Preservation Committee.
It is worth noting that the 1847
Gothic Revival church a few blocks
down Washington Street was also
decommissioned and is now the
Center for the Arts at the Chocolate
Church (Arthur D. Gilman, architect).

25

207 Main Street
Brunswick

Richard Upjohn, architect

The wooden Gothic has rarely been taken to such felicitous heights as in this church by the famous Richard Upjohn. The English-born architect is best known for his Trinity Church (1841–46) at the head of Wall Street in New York, but here (contemporaneous with Trinity) he produced a well-knit building that sympathetically holds down its traffic-heavy triangular site. The body of the church, with its light gray board-and-batten siding and lancet windows, is a simple statement of its Latin cross plan—narthex (in tower), nave, transepts, and chancel. The tower's "buttresses" step back as they rise, ending in a slatted belfry, pointed gables, and spiky pinnacles. Originally the church had a lofty spire (1848 but not by Upjohn) but this was destroyed in a gale in 1866 and—fortunately?—never replaced.

Whereas the exterior is merely comely, the interior revels in a fantastic forest of dark wood trusswork. It is perhaps unequaled for its technical and aesthetic bravura, with the lateral nave arches vigorously celebrating with the hammerbeam cross arches and the narrow ones spanning the side aisles. (It should be mentioned that steel tie-rods had to be added for stability following the storm of 1866.) The overall interior is on the dark side—the windows should have been larger—and there is a disturbing glare from the large window in the chancel, but First Parish is nonetheless a jewel. It was extensively renovated in 1968.

Incidentally, Upjohn's use of the "Gothic," an Anglican church form, initially upset many of First Parish's Congregationalists! For this job, it is illuminating to note, Upjohn was paid $250. He came to Brunswick only twice, once before beginning design to assess site and program and once as the church was nearing completion. He also designed at the same time the nearby, less satisfactory Bowdoin College Chapel of masonry.

Upjohn (1802–78) dedicated much of his life to improving the profession of architecture, not only helping to organize the American Institute of Architects but serving as its first president. His output both in churches and civil buildings is noteworthy.

HARRINGTON MEETINGHOUSE
[1772–75]

South on ME 129 8 mi/13 km, east
1.4 mi/2.1 km (or ME 130 via
Pemaquid)
Near Damariscotta

A first-rate meetinghouse which has
been carefully restored (1974) to its
original condition after suffering in-
dignities through the years. In 1775
it was dismantled and reassembled
on the present site, while in the
1840s it was again moved, this
time across its lot, then drastically
changed within and without. Today
it is handsomely maintained and
doubles as a museum. The church
is surrounded by an extensive and
well-landscaped cemetery on both
sides of the road with fine views to
the west. The overall form is good
while details of the entries are capably handled with pilasters at each
corner establishing the edges. The
upper windows break into the simple entablature. The interior is typically planned with balcony on three
sides and box pews, but the most
potent feature is the exposed roof
trussing which gives both interest
and space. The balcony level is now
used as a small local museum open
in July and August.

27

ELIJAH KELLOGG CHURCH [1843]

On ME 123
Harpswell Center

A naïve yet strangely sophisticated facade distinguishes this small "Village Gothic" church. Its double-door entry is framed by an eye-catching ogee arch that dominates the flush white-painted wood front. A local master joiner named Moses Bailey was the designer-carver. Double pilasters frame the whole, with tower, belfry, and spire, the latter with crockets, rising some 100 feet/30 m above. The interior is simple to the point of plainness. This village Congregational house of worship represents a fresh interpretation of the Gothic Revival in wood, a style which reached an ultimate in Upjohn's church just 8.5 mi/13 km to the north (25).

Directly across the street stands a typical meetinghouse from 1759—the oldest still standing in the state. It was used for religious and town functions until 1844, after which it served only the town. The interior has been changed to meet new needs.

28

FIRST PARISH UNITARIAN [1772/ 1804]

Portland Road at Summer
Kennebunk

A church in a historic village which serves as an urban pivot at its busy intersection. Its most prominent feature and the one which makes it a fulcrum is the square tower and its stages which project from the main mass of the church. These date from the 1804 addition and the basic alteration of the meetinghouse itself. The square open belfry supports an octagonal clock stage with nicely proportioned cornice. Atop this rises a small lantern (blank windows) with low dome and the usual weathervane. The tower and spire were added by Thomas Eaton, reputedly drawing on a design from Asher Benjamin's book, *The Country Builder's Assistant* (1797). At the same time the church was cut in two and 28 feet/8.5 m were added to the nave, moving the rear section back—and occasioning a few awkward junctures.

The most extraordinary feature of the interior is the second-floor worship room which has a clear span of approximately 70 feet/21 m. Its enormous (6,000 square feet/ 557 sq m) ceiling, which is hung from the roof trusses, is decorated with *trompe l'oeil* painting that overflows the side walls, including the "niches" in front. Its Greek Revival design was originally done with water-based paint but was replaced by oils in 1881 and fully restored in oil in 1979. Good urbanistically and startling within.

The Kennebunk heritage of substantial houses—built when the town was a noted shipbuilding center—is well worth exploring. The houses range in date from the mid eighteenth century to the end of the nineteenth.

A low-keyed, sensitive church, one of the finest small Roman Catholic churches in New England. A wall of local stone defines the parvis, while local wood walls and thick-butted, hand-split local shingles complete the materials. The walls are of vertical planking throughout, lightly bleached. An unusual "lantern" highlights the prominent roof and marks a ridge skylight. In plan the church is divided into two sections with worship room to right and social hall with kitchen at left. There is also a tiny chapel next to the sacristy.

The church room forms a square with altar in the center carrying out the Vatican II directives (1962–65). Daylighting comes from the ridge skylight mentioned and from the two sides, which are lined with alternating glass and wood panels (and at times producing a slight glare). Excellent downlights in the ceiling provide artificial illumination. All details, including those in the tiny chapel, were designed with refreshing directness. As the summer influx into the Mt. Desert area is considerable, the architect aligned the social hall with the nave to take care of overflow.

29

ST. PETER'S CHURCH [1967]

Southwest Harbor (Manset) on ME 102A
Mt. Desert

Willoughby M. Marshall, architect

30

ST. PATRICK'S CHURCH [1808]

Academy Road, 1.8 mi/3 km north
  of town
Newcastle

Nicholas Codd, builder-architect

A simple red brick church of Federal influence in design set in a rural area. It served the Catholics from Ireland who came to Maine in increasing numbers after the American Revolution; as the oldest Roman Catholic church in the state, it has offered mass since 1808. Its two-foot/61-cm thick walls are of local brick. The bell tower, with Paul Revere bell, was added in 1818, while the wood spire on top dates from 1866.

The nave is intimate, with five round-headed windows on either side, each with similar stained glass (added in 1896) and each with a Station of the Cross in the keystone above. The altar is unusual in its baroque shape, reputedly recalling those in France whence came the first priest. The painting above is of the Descent from the Cross. The bowed ceiling of the nave contributes to the atmosphere of quiet worshipfulness. The church was recently restored by J. Everette Fauber, Jr., who had worked at Williamsburg. St. Patrick's is listed in the National Register of Historic Places. The adjoining cemetery is also of interest.

FIRST PARISH CHURCH [1826]

425 Congress Street at Temple
Portland

A doughty city church at the head of
Temple Street, its rough-cut Maine
granite walls and slate roof giving it
the air of eternity. (It was indeed one
of the few buildings to survive Portland's Great Fire of 1866.) Its gabled
front is dominated by a projected
square tower slightly stepped in near
ridge line to emphasize the height.
The round heads of the three entries
are repeated above in a slightly
larger roundel and echoed at top
of tower by the circular clock. The
simplicity of the body of the facade
gives emphasis to the texture of the
granite and to the well-designed
louvered belfry, cupola, and spire,
which are of wood. A small yard
on either side of the church provides
a mid-urban breathing space. The
building is approximately 66 feet/20
m wide and 102 feet/31 m long.

The interior comprises one large
room with slightly arched ceiling
with niche behind the pulpit (original) and the usual balconies. A
prominent crystal chandelier (also
original) provides the chief focus but
the interior is not as compelling as
the facade. Some interior changes
were made in the middle of the last
century but these were "corrected"
in 1876. Upkeep and care since then
have been thorough.

32

SHAKER MEETINGHOUSE [1794]

Shaker Village
East off Exit 11 of Turnpike, north
  on ME 26 about 8 mi/13 km
Sabbathday Lake

This Shaker community (see also Hancock Shaker Village near Pittsfield, Massachusetts; 53) comprises sixteen wooden buildings and one brick dwelling dating from 1794 to 1847; of these, the Meetinghouse—now a museum—is the only one with architectural personality. The exterior has the gambrel roof with dormers seen at Hancock and the two entries—one for brethren, the other (and equal) for sisters—are similar. Inside, the ground floor is unobstructed to accommodate the sect's famous dancing, with apartments on the second. The simplicity of the interior is repeated in the marvelously sinewy benches and other furniture. "Purity" of design characterizes everything that came from these extraordinary celibate and "communistic" people (property was communal), whose industriousness and dedication were important factors in developing scientific agriculture and cattle breeding in the early nineteenth century. Moses Johnson of New Hampshire reportedly built this 1794 meetinghouse, plus a brace of others elsewhere in New England. Though the buildings of the United Society of Believers in Christ's Second Coming are not architecturally significant, Shaker furniture and tool design are proud heritages of our early culture.

Sabbathday Lake is the last active Shaker community. Though its members now number less than a dozen, it hopes to carry on into the next century.

33

OLD GERMAN CHURCH [1772]

West off ME 32, 1 mi/1.6 km south
    of US 1
Waldboro

The rewards of this small Lutheran church are to be found primarily in its bucolic setting and its seemingly infinite cemetery (dating from the 1700s) which stretches intriguingly up the small hill behind it, the whole embraced by a variety of trees. The light beige church itself is unusual for its eighteenth-century date in that the pulpit is at the long (i.e., narrow) end and the liturgical axis accented at the other end by the two-story projecting stair hall and entry. It measures approximately 30 feet/9.1 m by 45 feet/13.7 m. Most of the meeting-houses of this period had their entries in the long wall facing the pulpit. The compacted interior has gray painted box pews and a high handsome pulpit from the 1790s. Somewhat startlingly, the church, because of land claims, was moved in 1795 from its original site across the Medomak River—moved when the river was frozen—to its present site. The church was long abandoned but was repaired in 1872 and was recently restored; it is now well maintained.

Its early Lutheran congregation had come to this area of Maine from their native Germany in hopes of finding a better life; apparently most of them stayed on, but regrets can be read on some of the fascinating tombstones.

The Wiscasset area—which was probably visited by the Portuguese in the early sixteenth century and by the Vikings before that—developed into an important port and ship-building center in the eighteenth and early nineteenth centuries. The competition of railroads and steam-powered vessels eventually eroded the town's prosperity, leaving, however, a legacy of comely houses, church, courthouse, and a common which ranks high in Maine's attractions. Crowning the top of the Common are this white-painted church and brick courthouse (1824). The church, alas, burned in 1907 but was rebuilt, basically as it had been, in 1909. (The 1840 building was a similar but larger edition of a 1792 church.) Even the Revere bell, though melted, was partly incorporated in its replacement. The architecture of the church states with direct simplicity a coherence of porch, pediment, and steeple, the belfry and spire attended by lively finials. Note the doubled Ionic columns at the ends of the portico. The interior is of less interest; the overall atmosphere delightful.

34

FIRST CONGREGATIONAL
CHURCH [1840/1909]

The Common/US 1
Wiscasset

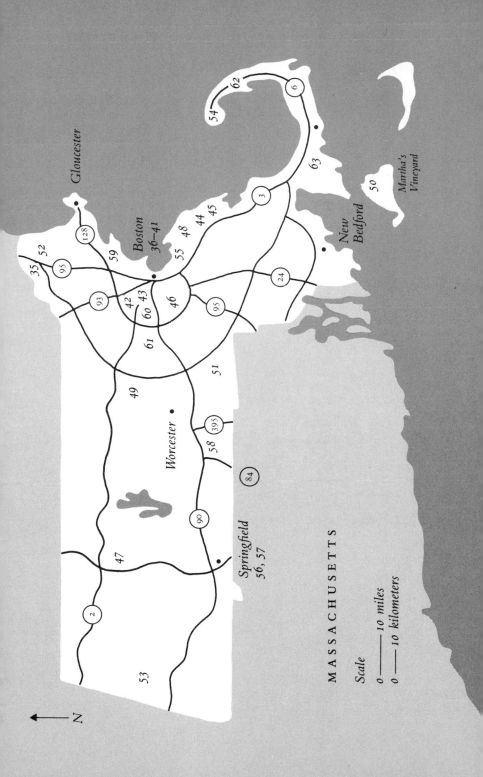

N

Gloucester

54
62
6
63
50 Martha's Vineyard

128
52
35
95
93
59
Boston
36–41
55
42
43
46
60
61
48
44
45
3
24
95
New
Bedford
51
49
Worcester
395
58
84
90
47
2
Springfield
56, 57
53

MASSACHUSETTS

Scale

0 ——— 10 miles
0 ——— 10 kilometers

ROCKY HILL MEETINGHOUSE
[1785]

Southeast out Elm Street, southeast
  of IS 495
Amesbury

Within a span of a dozen or so miles (20 km) are three of New England's finest meetinghouses: Danville (1760) and Sandown (1774), both in New Hampshire (67, 78), and Amesbury's Rocky Hill, just across the Massachusetts line. All three are vivid testimonials to the spartan setting for worship of two hundred years ago, when a minimum of two-hour services in unheated buildings was the norm. Fortunately, the three mentioned are now solicitously maintained, having been snatched from neglect and vandalism. Rocky Hill is larger and in some respects more accomplished than its cousins across the border; moreover, it is often open to the public in summer months. Directly behind stands the parsonage dating from around 1750 and moved to the present site in 1966.

The Rocky Hill Meetinghouse is a two-story gabled box, 61 feet/19 m wide by 49 feet/15 m deep, with a projected and well-pedimented vestibule and good framed entry (but undistinguished front door). No steeple—or chimney—interrupts its simple roof planes. The cornice, like the pediment of the projection, is well modillioned, though there is visual discomfort in the juncture of vestibule and front wall.

The interior breathes airy spaciousness, with forty-two windows, each containing sixteen over sixteen panes, encircling the worship room. Dominating the interior is the raised, paneled pulpit and sounding board: they attain almost regal proportions. Galleries surround three sides; seating capacity is almost 700. The box pews were left in their natural wood, now smoothed by years of usage, while naïve marbleizing on the supporting columns and on the pilasters framing the pulpit is the Puritan's rare concession to aesthetics. Town meetings ceased being held here in 1884—religious ones earlier—and for many years the deserted meetinghouse was in danger of collapse. Acquisition by the Society for the Preservation of New England Antiquities in 1936 and subsequent restoration saved a glorious statement from our past.

36

CHRIST CHURCH / OLD NORTH
[1723]

193 Salem Street or via Paul Revere
  Mall on Hanover Street
Boston

The early settlers of the Massachusetts Bay Colony were not Separatists from the Church of England.
However, with their religious re-
form efforts being rebuffed in England, they organized in America a
theocratic government which did
not tolerate any faith but their own
"purified" creed. These Puritans
"pointed out that they had founded
a religious colony and that it was not
right to expect them to admit possible subversive elements" (*Massachusetts State Guide,* Houghton Mifflin,
1971). The Plymouth Colony Pilgrims, on the other hand, were
fiercely independent Separatists.
They brought Congregationalism—
founded in England in 1582—to the
New World, eventually (1692) meld-
ing with the Congregationalists in
the Massachusetts Bay Colony. Thus
it was not until the late seventeenth
century—amid strenuous objections—that the first Anglican parish
was established in Boston and a
wooden church built (1688). Roman
Catholics were initially banned from
the colony. (It is useful to remember
that the Virginia Colony—to which
the Pilgrims were originally headed
until blown off course—was Church
of England from its founding in
1607. Roman Catholics, incidentally,
helped settle Maryland as early as
1634.)

Old North, as it is familiarly
known from Longfellow's poem,
represents a splendid architectural
beginning for the Church of England
in New England—after the Revolution renamed the Protestant Episcopal Church—and was of substantial
influence in the northern colonies
(see Trinity Church in Newport,
R.I.; 84). The present structure ac-
tually was the second church for its
congregation, an earlier one having
been outgrown, but it was the first
constructed of brick. For guidance
in its design its founders naturally
looked to London for inspiration,

thus to the works of Christopher Wren (1632–1723) and his successor James Gibbs (1682–1754). Strangely, however, no specific name of architect or master carpenter has been found for Old North's final appearance in spite of copious surviving church records. (The National Register of Historic Places lists William Price as the designer.)

Old North today is hemmed in by nondescript neighbors and the most agreeable approach is via the well-landscaped Paul Revere Mall (1930s). The exterior of the church forms a brick rectangle, 51½ feet/15.7 m wide by 71 feet/22 m long, with gabled roof and prominent tower and spire (familiar, of course, to Paul Revere) surveying the north end of Boston from its highest hill. The evolution of the design of the 195-foot/59-m high steeple is of interest in that it was blown down during a hurricane in 1804, redesigned by Charles Bulfinch two years later, toppled by another hurricane in 1954, and replaced that same year, using, it is thought, the eighteenth-century design of William Price. For 150 years an ill-scaled clock stage (Bulfinch?) had dominated the tower. Elegance now prevails.

The surprising impression on entering the church—a retreat from its surroundings—is one of verticality. This is intensified by the commanding height of the arched niche of the sanctuary with its Great Window, and by the columns upholding the galleries and their vaults. The bays marked by the square columns, paneled below the balconies and fluted above, create a series of cross axes, their small vaults reflecting the vaulted ceiling of the nave to create a three-dimensional groined interplay. It is an alive space. Adding to the attractions of the 42-foot/13-m high nave are two brass chandeliers (1724) and a particularly well-turned wine-glass pulpit with airily suspended sounding board. The apsidal sanctuary is unusual in having a painting of Jesus at the Last Supper (by James

Penniman, 1812) flanked by panels bearing the Ten Commandments, Apostle's Creed, and the Lord's Prayer. (Such panels were often seen in churches of the middle and southern colonies of this time, primarily because of the scarcity of prayer books.) The altar forms a simple block seasonally vested. The windows throughout are of plain glass, both for better light to follow the service (cf. the sombrous Gothic Revival churches of the mid nineteenth century) and to afford "a view of the outside world," as the church booklet mentions.

The interior which we see today is the result of a wholesale restoration undertaken in 1912. Throughout much of the nineteenth century the church was increasingly sullied: the Great Window was walled up, the wineglass pulpit removed, center aisle omitted and, worst of all, the whole inside was floridly painted with false drapery, swags, and artless decorations. Both interior and exterior are now in pristine condition.

Note: Across from the Paul Revere Mall at 401 Hanover Street stands St. Stephen's Roman Catholic Church, built in 1802 to a design by Bulfinch for the Congregational Church. It was sold to the Catholic diocese in 1862 and considerably altered within. Bulfinch's use of the dome instead of spire was unusual for a church; it stemmed from his State House of 1798.

OLD SOUTH MEETINGHOUSE
[1730]

Washington Street at Milk
Boston

Robert Twelves, designer

As the eighteenth century began and
New England towns burgeoned, the
need for larger houses of worship
began to be felt. The basically
square, hipped-roof meetinghouses
of the seventeenth century could not
readily be expanded for structural
reasons, thus the oblong plan with
entry on the long side opposite the
pulpit evolved as here in Old South.
However, it should be kept in mind
that the relatively few Anglican
churches of this period—as opposed
to Congregational meetinghouses—
almost always followed the longitudinal plan seen in Christ Church/Old
North (36) with entry at the end facing the altar. Later in the eighteenth
century and as the 1800s progressed,
virtually all houses of worship took
the longitudinal plan, the meetinghouse, as has been said, becoming a
church.

Old South, initially the third Congregational Church, was one of the
first of the Type II meetinghouses
and also one of the earliest to be
built of brick. (Dr. Edmund W. Sinnott in his admirable book *Meetinghouse and Church in Early New
England* [McGraw-Hill, 1963]
describes four stages or "Types" of
development: Type I, the squarish
structures of the mid and late seventeenth century; Type II, 1710–1800,

with entry on long side opposite pulpit as here; Type III, 1800–1820s, longitudinal with portico and door at end; and Type IV, after 1825, the beginning of the revival period.) Old South, which measures 94 feet/29 m wide by 67 feet/20 m deep, forms a sturdy landmark in midtown Boston, its square tower cleverly tied to the block of the building by two stringcourses and by the repetition of round-headed windows. Note the upper tower window, the oculus above, and the round head of the louvered belfry, here with bells in the tower itself. On top, behind a prominent balustrade, rises an octagonal cupola which fairs into a spire with eight "dormers" at its base. The original entry, now closed, was in the center of the long wall facing the pulpit, as mentioned. It still retains its portico.

There is an open forum, almost theater, quality about the interior, stemming primarily from the double galleries on the sides with raked seats—the upper primarily meant for slaves—which focus on the elaborate pulpit (not original). During the Revolution, Old South was gutted by the British and used as a riding school. It was eventually restored following peace (1783) and again in 1857, but the last religious services were held in 1872, the congregation seeking new quarters. For a few years it served as a post office. Then in 1876 the building was offered for sale, the land being valuable, and it was scheduled to be torn down. Through the valiant efforts of concerned citizens, primarily women, a private subscription was raised to acquire Old South, one of the city's most historic sites (the Boston Tea Party started here) and make it into a museum.

58 Tremont Street at School
Boston

Peter Harrison, architect

King's Chapel, built—despite Puritan objections—in the prosperous days of the Massachusetts Colony during the French and Indian War, is one of the most important churches in New England. The exterior with its granite walls and its dark, almost uninviting portico (finished 1787—columns of wood) sets a stern entry, but the interior glows with a welcoming grandeur. An elaborate spire was originally designed to climax the tower but funds ran out. Even without steeple, however, the church creates a powerful image as one approaches it from Tremont Street, its mass almost bristling in its compaction. (The influence of James Gibbs's *A Book of Architecture* [1728] can be seen.) A small cemetery (1630s) adjacent to the north side gives the church a modicum of breathing space in today's urban anarchy. Harrison's considerable mathematical skills are evident in the plan of the church whereby the nave's proportions reflect those of a side of a square to its diagonal: approximately 58 feet/17.7 m wide by 83 feet/25 m long, while the height of the nave is half its width. Other mathematical relationships—pitch of roof, height of sill of tower opening, etc.—also were design determinants, factors made popular by Palladio in the six-

teenth century and epitomized by Le Corbusier's Modulor in the twentieth.

The interior, as mentioned, is resplendent. The paired and fluted two-story Corinthian columns, upholding the lateral galleries as they march imperially down the aisle, set a powerful introduction to the prominent pulpit with sounding board (from the old church of 1717). Behind in a shallow apse (Harrison was limited by contract to 10 feet/ 3 m) rises the well-lit but somewhat restless sanctuary. The four black plaques present the Apostle's Creed, the Lord's Prayer, and the Ten Commandments. The four busts are of the first Unitarian ministers of the church, Unitarians having won most of the congregation (1780s) when Church of England services ceased because of the Revolution. King's Chapel then became the first Unitarian Church in America. Changes in the interior have been comfortably minimal: five painted glass windows were installed in the 1860s but only one remains, the governor's pew adjudged undemocratic in 1826 was removed but rebuilt in 1928, and the organ has several times been spruced up. King's Chapel otherwise is as Peter Harrison designed it: one could scarce ask for more.

39

TRINITY CHURCH [1877/1897]

Copley Square
Boston

H. H. Richardson, architect

From some viewpoints the formidable bulk of Trinity Church can be confusing: the relation of the enormous tower to the body of the church is not immediately graspable, while the tower's profusion of windows and blind openings leaves one uncertain as to what goes on inside. However, doubts vanish when the church is seen from the square in front, for here one experiences a synthesis of rambunctious elements and a scale build-up of prodigious proportions. The church, the commission for which was won by competition, fortunately underwent many design changes before being finished (350 design studies still exist).

Richardson was the second American (after Richard Morris Hunt) to graduate from Paris's Ecole des Beaux Arts, and in his six years abroad he traveled widely in Europe. His chief delight was in visiting the Romanesque architecture of central and south France and in Spain (did his Louisiana birth nurture these southern preferences?) and churches in both of these countries influenced the design of Trinity. The projected portal recalls the church at Saint-Gilles (A.D. 1150), while the clustered ripple of arches can be seen in Poitiers (eleventh century), among others, and the use of stone polychromy has several French sources. The famous square tower which anchors the church (it was octagonal and awkward in early sketches) derives in part from Spain's Cathedral of Salamanca, about 1200. Richardson was—as were the times—eclectic, but he himself was always independent. He might even have resented being known as the father of Richardsonian Romanesque. Trinity's portal, it should be noted, was not completed until 1897 (by Shepley, Rutan & Coolidge) basically to HHR's design, Richardson having died in 1886 at the age of forty-eight.

Trinity forms a modified Greek cross in plan, its four arms framing the towered crossing. They also bring the congregation into greater liturgical intimacy than an attenuated Latin-cross plan. The transepts form rectangles twice as wide as deep, while the span of the crossing (e.g., the tower) is approximately twice their depth, being thus 1–2–1 in modules. The outside width of transept to transept is 121 feet/36.9 m. The tower (211 feet/64 m) rests on 4,500 piles on its landfill site. The impact of the interior stuns under the stupendous crossing which vanishes 103 feet/31 m upward to a coffered ceiling, with the four barrel vaults of the "arms" lurking behind dramatic tie-rods which create horizontal tension. Note that the vaults, which are of elaborately stenciled wood, do not span the wall-to-wall width but rest on short half-vaults, a compounding of the curves which adds to the geometric zest. However, the excitement of the interior's three dimensions is almost lost in the encompassing refulgence of its walls. Their decoration was the collaborative effort of John La Farge, the famous New York-born artist, working closely with Richardson and assistants (including the British Pre-Raphaelite Edward Burne-Jones). Employing all surfaces of the interior as their canvas, they stenciled walls, painted murals, and worked with stained glass to create a "color church" of dazzling homogeneity, intensity, and warm beauty. The result was the first major collaboration of architect and artist in church architecture in the United States. For many observers the interior is not equaled on this continent. The chancel was redecorated in 1938 by Charles D. Maginnis and the nave restored in 1957.

40

CHRISTIAN SCIENCE CENTER
[1972]

Huntington Avenue at Massachusetts
Boston

I. M. Pei & Associates, architects

One of the difficult problems confronting the architects in the design of this vast extension of the Christian Science complex was to create urban coherence in a once-blighted part of the city while being sympathetic to the mother church of 1894 and its major extension of 1905. Pei and his associates stabilized the area with a 670-foot/204-m long reflecting pool, backed it with a colonnaded building that plays with light and shade, anchored it with a twenty-eight-story administration tower, and gave it punctuation with a low but prominent Sunday School unit. The original church, of Romanesque inspiration (Franklin Welch architect), seats approximately 1,000 worshipers; it is still used for some services. This was soon outgrown and the enormous Byzantine-Renaissance church, seating 3,000, was added in 1905 (Charles Brigham chief architect).

For the 1972 expansion the architects designed a tower to establish an equilibrium with the churches across the reflecting pool, (2 feet/.6 m deep), placing a 550-car garage underneath, and called on the colonnade's bold geometry to hold all together. Cafeteria, reading room, and services occupy the colonnade building. The Sunday School contains forty classrooms and an auditorium seating 1,100. The Center's counterpoint of vertical tower and horizontal pool—the spirited and the calm—represents a first-rate urban solution to a difficult problem while splendidly serving administrative needs.

First and Second (combined in 1970) is no ordinary church, nor would one expect such from one of architecture's most imaginative practitioners. The previous church (1868) on the site—a block from Boston Common—burned in 1968 but its stone tower and spire were left intact. Though there was spirited discussion as to what should be done with the ruins, sentiment ran heavily toward preserving the century-old tower. Paul Rudolph fully agreed and used it to anchor the east end of his new building. In seeking to respond to the domestic scale and character of the neighborhood, the architect set the body of the church back from the sidewalk and inserted a partially sunken, open-air amphitheater as intermedium between street and building. A small garage was somewhat prominently placed in the lowest level.

One enters the church via a purposefully narrow ramp to come into a welcoming double-height lobby. From there, one proceeds to the sanctuary via another constrained passage to burst into the worship room. This "spiral route" of open-squeeze-open reflects Rudolph's interest in a calculated circulation whose goal is to make space a vital experience. The sanctuary continues this spatial enthusiasm—almost no side walls are parallel, no ceiling planes are horizontal, and few right angles are in sight. The planes which create this sculpted space vividly interact to produce an exciting nave: it is washed by light, natural and artificial, seen and unseen, throughout the day. The nave is on the narrow and perhaps restless side, and the angled organ (made in Germany) overly dominant, but the church represents an intriguing exercise in three very vital dimensions. A 220-seat auditorium with small stage—often used by a local college—is situated next to the tower. (The church makes its spaces available to a number of neighborhood organizations.) A chapel, classrooms, and administrative facilities complete the project.

FIRST AND SECOND CHURCH
UNITARIAN UNIVERSALIST [1972]

66 Marlborough Street
Boston

Paul Rudolph, architect

CHRIST CHURCH [1761]

Garden Street, on the Common
Cambridge

Peter Harrison, architect

The Old Burying Ground (1636) provides an apposite setting for this "pleasantly unconventional" church (Historic American Building Survey) with its fresh yet sophisticated wooden sides. Its round-headed windows, their arch springpoints laced together by a slender ornamental band (note its midpoint breaks), set an undulating rhythm, the whole topped by a broad but discreet cornice, the frieze emphasized by triglyphs. (These recall Harrison's Redwood Library in Newport, R.I., of 1750.) The roof is of two parallel but separate planes to keep its scale from dominating the side. Only the tower-belfry which projects in front is in disharmony: it appears to be tacked onto the body of the church. Some authorities believe that Harrison himself had little to do with the tower we see today. (Changes might well have been made during the basic repairs of 1790 following severe damage to the church during the Revolution.)

Peter Harrison (1716–75) was a brilliant, English-born amateur architect who was also responsible for King's Chapel in Boston (38) and Touro Synagogue in Newport (85). The history of Christ Church—and its architecture—was initially "inauspicious" since it was Church of England in a Puritan community. Moreover, its building funds were "impossibly low." As the American Revolution approached, not only were the minister and his Tory constituents forced to leave Cambridge (1774), the church building itself was taken over by townspeople, used as a barracks, and eventually vandalized.

It was not until 1790 that Christ Church was reopened, and not until 1825 that thorough repairs, outside and in, were made. Isaiah Rogers (1800–1869), a well-known Massachusetts-born architect, was in charge, and he not only secured the church, he changed Harrison's simple Doric columns resting on the floor into Ionic columns on pew-height plinths, and capped them with elaborate entablature blocks.

All of the remaining box pews were then made into slip pews. Rogers also detailed the "complementary decorative pilasters on the walls" (church folder). The chancel, an arc in plan, uses a large Palladian motif as retable. The plan measured 45 feet/13.7 m wide by 60 feet/18.2 m long.

By 1857 the church, having prospered, was cut in half and two additional bays were inserted between the original third and fourth bays, adding two windows to each side, an expansion anticipated by Harrison himself as indicated by timber joints. George Snell was the architect in charge of this expansion, and it is of interest to note that Snell also added (1858) to Harrison's above-mentioned library in Newport.

The interior of Christ Church, though suffering many changes through the years, as we have seen, today is impressive. The ceiling is deeply coved and embellished by two crystal chandeliers (1935), while the two side-aisle ceilings are flat. Handsome columns mark the divisions. A prominent cornice surrounds the interior—note that there are no galleries—while Harrison's cadence of round-headed windows with shutters develops an almost mathematical progression toward the chancel. In 1883 a Victorian "modernization" with "rich colors" took place, but the entire interior was properly restored to its near-original condition in the 1920s with minor alterations in the 1940s. As is evident, the interior we see today is the product of two distinguished architects, not Harrison alone. The overall result, however, is a very handsome Georgian church.

43

MIT CHAPEL [1955]

Off Massachusetts Avenue and
    Amherst Street
Cambridge

Eero Saarinen, architect

The MIT Chapel is not so much a setting for organized religion, though this can take place, as it is a retreat, a personal sanctuary where one can meditate or worship alone. (For organized services it can accommodate 130 people.) Moreover, the late Eero Saarinen (1910–61) wanted an embracing plan to intensify the relation of the individual to the altar. To this end he designed the chapel as a cylinder but with undulating interior walls—curved for both acoustic and aesthetic reasons—and he then surrounded the exterior with a circular pool to emphasize detachment. The outside walls, which measure 54 feet/16 m in diameter, rest on low arches in this moat and have on the inside a horizontal "light band" (2 feet 10 in/.9 m) around the chapel's periphery. Though windowless to screen out street and campus noises, the interior nonetheless receives light reflected from the pool throughout much of the day. (There is, however, too little light from this source.) The main illumination comes from a round skylight which cascades a dramatic flood of daylight over the altar and the superb gold-flecked screen behind it. The altar itself is a simple cube of polished marble offset on three circular steps of travertine: it can be used plain or with cross, menorah, or other religious symbol, accommodating a variety of faiths or no faiths at all. The screen behind the altar, its shining rectangular chips seemingly climbing to heaven, was designed by sculptor Harry Bertoia in close cooperation with the architect, who himself had once studied sculpture. It is one of the great works of twentieth-century religious art. The aluminum bell-spire on top was designed by Theodore Roszak. This gloriously sensitive chapel was one of Eero Saarinen's favorite works; he was buried from it, tragically young.

44

FIRST PARISH CHURCH AND
MEETINGHOUSE [1747]

On the Common
Cohasset

The historic towns threaded along
the Massachusetts coast are not only
generally delightful in themselves,
they gave birth to the settlement of
much of New England as newcom-
ers landed, then pushed on for available land. Even Connecticut was
initially settled (Hartford, Windsor,
Wethersfield) from Massachusetts,
not the sea. Cohasset, whose site
was visited by Captain John Smith
in 1614—six years before the Plymouth Colony settlers arrived on the
Mayflower—is one of these comely
towns properly focused on its spacious and almost casual Common.
Many authorities feel that Captain
Smith—of Pocahontas fame—was
also the first to call the area New
England. Until 1770 a semi-ne-
glected farming and fishing village
attached to Hingham, Cohasset is
now almost an adjunct of Boston, 17
miles/27 km away; mercifully it is
still unspoiled.

The First Parish, the second meetinghouse on the Common (the initial
one, ca. 1717, having been outgrown
and dismantled), measures 60 feet/
18 m wide by 45 feet/13.7 m deep.
It follows the "standard" meetinghouse pattern of the mid eighteenth
century, with gabled box form, projected entry (1768) in the middle of
the long side opposite the pulpit, and
bell tower (1799) at one end. The
square tower carries clocks on four
sides and is topped by an octagonal
open belfry behind balustrade, with
an octagonal spire and weather vane
above.

The interior, which is open most
mornings, focuses on an unusually
handsome pulpit: box pews add to
the general atmosphere. Unfortunate
changes in the 1800s have now been
corrected. One of the oldest Unitarian Universalist churches in New
England, it—and its setting—epito-
mize its era.

45

ST. STEPHEN'S EPISCOPAL
CHURCH [1900]

16 Highland Avenue at Main
Cohasset

Cram, Goodhue & Ferguson, architects

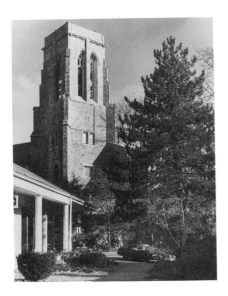

Ralph Adams Cram (1863–1942) and Bertrand C. Goodhue (1869–1924), both born in New England, were two of the most important American architects at the end of the nineteenth century and in the early decades of the twentieth. From 1891 to 1910 they joined their considerable talents to become Cram, Goodhue & Ferguson, the last named a distinguished engineer. Upon winning the competition for the rebuilding of the Cadet Chapel at West Point in 1903, the firm was catapulted into national prominence, particularly as regards religious work, in which both Cram and Goodhue had long been interested.

Cram especially was almost totally immersed in church architecture; as he once remarked, "religion is the essence of human life." In his practice he heralded the Gothic—serious medieval Gothic—as the only proper shelter for worship, particularly the "mysterious" setting for Communion. (Compare this with the Congregational/Universalist emphasis on the Word.) Though his father was a Unitarian minister, Cram was strictly a High Church Anglican. It is not certain that he "would have us living in walled towns . . . dragging the stones to the rising cathedral, yoked to wooden carts" (Thomas E. Tallmadge, *The Story of Architecture in America,* [Norton, 1936]), but he was the high priest of an architectural direction that gave a powerful imprimatur to religious building in this country, one whose vestiges can still be seen.

It must be remembered that this was a time—not unlike the present—of rampant eclecticism in architecture. The Richardsonian Romanesque had recently been superseded by the Neoclassic of the 1893 Chicago Fair and ambivalence ruled. Moreover, the protagonists of the Gothic could point to the greatest monuments of Christianity for their inspiration. That the cathedrals of more than half a millennium ago were built for a totally different culture, often with different materials, and generally for a different religion, was secondary to their undeniably dramatic setting for worship.

It should also be noted that architecture's nineteenth- and twentieth-century flirtation with the "Gothic" took several forms. "Early Gothic Revival" began in the first decades of the nineteenth century—see Trinity Church in New Haven of 1816 (15)—and continued until the Greek Revival (1820s and '30s) took over, followed by an Italian (basically Tuscan) Revival. Around the mid nineteenth century "Victorian Gothic" appeared on the scene, a period of superficial reasonableness, plus occasional polychromy, molding churches as well as houses. Many handsome churches resulted, but Gothic was mostly in their skins as steel buttressed their piers and suspended their ceilings, and in many cases their "flying buttresses," though visible, flew nowhere. The Gothic which Cram advocated and which he stuck to "with unshaken rigidity" represented a return to a medieval stone-on-stone authenticity, with structural purity and superb craftsmanship. Cram, in his *American Church Building of Today* (Architectural Book Publishing Company, 1929), even wrote that "no contribution was made to Christian art after this [pre-Reformation, i.e., Gothic] period." As the twentieth century progressed such goals became elusive.

Among the most accomplished smaller churches which Cram, Goodhue & Ferguson designed is St. Stephen's, crowning a hillock in this pleasant town and within sight of First Parish Meetinghouse on the Common. A commanding, well-buttressed tower with carillon (1928) dominates the granite massing and stabilizes the courtyard on entrance side. The tall and narrow nave finds climax in the raised sanctuary, above which shines a large stained-glass window. Six memorial windows line the nave but the overall level of daylight is low. Sunday school rooms and administrative quarters are grouped around the court. Sui generis, thoroughly professional.

46

FIRST CHURCH, UNITARIAN
[1761/1820]

674 High Street
Dedham

A bold, slightly disjointed geometry characterizes the facade of First Church. The vertically emphasized projected entry bay with four tall pilasters (and two curiously paneled doors) is topped by the usual pediment, here featuring a half-round window with tracery. The tower with clock rises directly behind but in front of the gabled block of the nave. A square belfry with framed round-headed opening on each side (reflecting the front doors), pilasters at the corners, entablature around top, and urns on the edges, supports the square lantern, which is a stretched edition of the belfry. A simple octagonal spire tops all with its own set of corner urns, here prominent against the sky. The three stages of urns play an important role in the perkiness of the facade. It is pertinent to point out that the height of the belfry, lantern, and spire is precisely that of the front to tip of pediment.

The atmosphere of the interior is cordial, indeed almost domestic. This is accentuated by the plum-colored cloth which covers the pews, including their backs, and by the white trim and gray walls. The most unusual feature of the worship room is the triple-arched recessed and paneled chancel with projecting pulpit. A simple altar stands in front. On either side—and adding to the domesticity—are portraits of outstanding parish ministers. The detailing of the galleries and the cornice is good throughout.

The present appearance of First Church stems from the heavy remodeling of 1820 when a congregational schism occurred. At this time "the roof was turned to run east and west, the east side was extended and the present steeple built facing the east" (church bulletin).

The First Church should not be regarded alone but as a major embellishment to this historic and gloriously preserved village. The church gives accent to the mile-long "Street," architecturally recalling other Federal Style churches with its graceful recessed arches parading along its brick walls. (See similar churches in Newport, N.H. [75] and New Haven, Conn. [16].) The square wooden tower doubles as a belfry topped by the usual octagonal stages. A weather vane, here a cock from the 1731 meetinghouse, supervises all. The tower is not as sophisticated as the rest of the exterior.

The interior, most of which can be seen through the windows, "recalls the seventeenth-century Puritan plain style. The cold rationalism of the earlier Puritans was apparently to some extent congenial to the Deerfield Unitarians" (*A Brief History of Deerfield*, 1972). The interior is thus extremely simple: other than the removal of mid-nineteenth-century plaques no changes have been made.

Deerfield was a lonely frontier village when founded in 1655 in what is now called the Connecticut Valley. Its inhabitants having been twice massacred in clashes with Native Americans (1669, 1704), a determined effort was made to preserve Deerfield's heritage. In 1952 this was given rewarding testament when Mr. and Mrs. Henry N. Flynt created Historic Deerfield as a nonprofit organization to maintain twelve house-museums open to the public. Don't miss.

47

THE FIRST CHURCH [1824]

The Street
Deerfield

Winthrop Clapp, designer

48

OLD SHIP MEETINGHOUSE
[1681, 1729, 1755]

Main Street
Hingham

As the only surviving seventeenth-century New England meetinghouse, Old Ship is of singular importance: it is also the oldest wooden church in this country and claims to be the oldest in continuous use. (This last disputed by St. Luke's Church in Isle of Wight County, Virginia.) Architecturally Old Ship is fascinating. Though alongside a busy avenue, it is placed back from it to establish presence; trees and a cemetery provide backdrop. As indicated by the dates above, the church evolved in several stages and it was not until 1755 that it took the form we see today. The original core of 1681 measures 45 feet/13.7 m wide by 55 feet/16.7 m deep and had the pulpit on the center of its right-hand wall opposite the then main entrance. In 1729 a 14-foot/4.3-m expansion was made on this right (northeast) side, the pulpit moved to the present site, and in 1755 a similar addition was made on the opposite side. A new roof was obviously needed to cover the two additions; this was done by a hipped roof similar to the original but with a subtle upturn of the ridges near the corners. A flat balustraded deck on top supports an open octagonal belfry with imaginative steeple crowning all. The two projected entries or vestibules date from the 1755 addition.

Whereas the exterior and its evolution are of interest, the interior is staggering under the exposed trusswork of its roof. The three prodigious trusses with curved struts which span the 45-foot/13.7-m width of the original worship space are a mighty testament to seventeenth-century wood engineering, their upturned hull-like shape giving the church its name. It should be noted that only the original 45 by 55-foot (13.7 × 16.7 m) core is roofed with the sinewy beams: the two lateral additions have flat ceilings. A handsome pulpit with twin windows behind gives focus to the room. The meetinghouse being heatless, a flat ceiling was installed in 1731 reducing air volume, this preserved both parishioners and trusses.

The usual renovations and changes beset Old Ship through the years: in 1791 the congregation voted to tear it down as being dowdy compared to churches in the newly fashionable "Wren Style." With the whole ceiling plastered over, the interior must indeed have been dullish; moreover, the building needed repair. Needless to say, the vote was rescinded the next year. Then in 1869 the inevitable Victorian influence was felt, the interior was ornately decorated and curved benches replaced the box pews. Beginning in the 1930s, however, a total restoration to its original condition was undertaken by architect Edgar T. P. Walker and the splendid results are here for all to enjoy. Superb.

49

FIRST CHURCH OF CHRIST [1817]

The Common
Lancaster

Charles Bulfinch, architect

Presiding with patrician aplomb over the lovely Town Common, the Federal Style First Church also delights with some of the most elegant proportions in religious architecture. It was designed by Bulfinch and his housewright-associate Thomas Hearsey. The projected porch consists of three knife-sliced brick arches in front and one on each side—all equal. The arches are divided by white-painted Doric pilasters doubling as exclamation points, with a proper entablature and pediment binding all together. It is illuminating to note that Bulfinch's original design of the church shows a portico with tall central opening flanked by two shorter ones, the size of the lower ones reflecting the vestibule doors under the porch (*Old Time New England*, April 1937). As Bulfinch reputedly never visited the site, it is inescapable that Hearsey as job captain was responsible for making the three arches equal. Whereas most of us would joyfully applaud the results, one critic carped on "the rather uninspired monotony of the three equal sized arches." De gustibus!

A square brick tower rises above and behind the portico at the front edge of the building proper. The fan-shaped buttresses which wed the tower to the block of the church were also suggestions made by Hearsey. Resting on the tower is a temple-like cylindrical belfry, wrapped by twelve Ionic columns topped by a smart entablature. This is crowned by a smaller cylinder, or attic, whose gray wooden form is made cheerful by white swags. A white dome and weather vane top all at 120 feet/ 37 m. The imagination of Bulfinch's detailing and the subtle use of gray and white above the red Lancaster brick are impeccable, while the overall freshness of design adds a sophisticated note to nineteenth-century religious architecture.

The interior, which measures 66 feet/20 m wide by 74 feet/23 m long, forms a simple, slightly dry worship room whose main accent is an almost regal pulpit supported by eight Ionic columns. A rich green curtain "from a Parisian model" fills the arched opening behind the minister. Doric columns support the full-length galleries on both sides. In 1869 almost all the congregation except the minister wanted to divide the church into two floors, using the upper for worship and the lower for parish and related needs: fortunately the popular divine prevailed. A chapel was attached to the north end in 1881, necessitating the closure of several windows in the pulpit wall, the interior was frescoed, and two large plaques placed beside the pulpit (they are now on the rear wall). The well-scaled ceiling decoration dates from 1900. At the end of the last century the exterior suffered superficial indignity when the pilasters, entablature, and belfry were painted dark brown. The entire church has been beautifully restored (1987) and is now in excellent condition. Its location at the end of a relaxed green adds greatly to its pleasure.

50

WESLEYAN GROVE CAMPGROUND
AND TABERNACLE [1879]

Oak Bluffs
Martha's Vineyard

J. W. Hoyt, architect

During the Great Awakening of the eighteenth century George White-field (1714–70), the famous English Methodist minister, made a number of evangelistic trips to the Colonies (he died in Exeter, New Hampshire), drawing enormous crowds. His spirit of group revivalism came to life again almost a century later and in 1835 the Wesleyan Grove Camp Meeting was inaugurated as a Methodist summer assembly. (There were, reputedly, seven others in Massachusetts alone.) The early settlements on this island five miles/ eight km off the coast of Cape Cod were on the primitive straw-and-tent side, but after the Civil War "Cottage City" was platted (1880), to be renamed Oak Bluffs in 1907. Its twenty acres lie seven miles/eleven km north of Edgartown. The hundreds of tents eventually gave way to fantastic lines of cottages, almost all of them 11 to 16 feet/3.4–4.9 m wide, all intimately side by side, and all with gables facing the various streets and greens. In time, most of them added fanciful ginger-bread front porches which improved internal privacy and encouraged external gregariousness. Well over 300 of these often gaily painted cottages remain, a number of them winterized and occupied throughout the year. The land, it should be noted, still belongs to the Martha's Vineyard Campmeeting Association.

The focus of Wesleyan Grove is the 2,000-capacity Tabernacle, a technically daring, little-known, open-sided structure of T-irons and pipes upholding rafters, topped by a corrugated roof. It was "assembled in several weeks of the summer of 1879 by George Dwight, a Springfield dealer in galvanized iron and builder of fireproof buildings, and his partner, John Hoyt, a campground resident" (*Architecture Plus*, November 1973). The Massachusetts Historical Commission lists J. W. Hoyt as architect. The structure measures 130 feet/40 m across, its two set-backs rising to a central height of 100 feet/30 m. Although primarily a protection from heat and rain more than a formal "house of worship," the Tabernacle sheltered thousands of the faithful attending sermons, prayers, and hymn-singings—events which often generated a "quickening" among its followers as the religious tempo increased through the day. Today it is also gratefully used by the community. A homely but remarkable structure.

51

UNITARIAN CHURCH [1820]

Maple Street at Elm
Mendon

Elias Carter, architect

The village of Mendon, some 38 miles/61 km southwest of Boston, had early Colonial roots, being settled in 1660, and in many respects this church reflects both roots and village architecture. Designed by Elias Carter (1783–1864), who was prominent in central Massachusetts and New Hampshire (see his churches in Fitzwilliam and Hancock; 69, 71), the church—the fifth since Mendon was founded—forms a solid example. It is also a mirror of its parish which felt that the old meetinghouse was "getting dilapidated and also entirely out of fashion, having no spire, tower, or bell" (church bulletin). Mr. Carter responded sympathetically to the commission. He produced a new church whose basic simplicity is given restrained accents by the projected porch with four stretched Tuscan columns, three doors, half-round-topped windows above and Palladian window in center. The half-rounds are echoed in the pediment, tower, and octagonal belfry and lantern, a shingled spire topping all at 130 feet/ 40 m.

The interior is simple, light, and airy with a minimum of embellishment except for the pulpit and its enthusiastically pilastered "framing." In 1936 lightning struck and the ensuing fire destroyed tower, spire, and the southeast corner. With the generous help of the American Unitarian Association and friends, a complete restoration was effected.

52

FIRST RELIGIOUS SOCIETY [1801]

26 Pleasant Street
Newburyport

Newburyport's harbor facilities on the Merrimack River were once so flourishing that its shipping and shipbuilding yards almost rivaled Boston's. Thomas Jefferson's Embargo Act of 1807 stunted commerce, a fire leveled the heart of the city in 1811, and the advent of steam power made its famous clipper ships obsolescent, while the harbor clogged with sand. However, the city has bequeathed us a splendid collection of eighteenth- and nineteenth-century buildings, largely Federal in style, including this particularly handsome church. Today Newburyport is vigorously preserving and restoring its past as it monitors its future (with, perhaps, too little concern for what the automobile is erasing).

The church is tightly hemmed in and the best approach is from the landscaped lot behind. The facade is characterized by fine-tuned detailing albeit with several scale puzzlements.

Among these is the distracting tension of the doors and windows in the two side bays of the three-bay front: their width sets up competition with the center. Moreover, the height of the square tower is excessive for its well-turned steeple. As recompense, so to speak, Ralph Adams Cram, the famous church architect, termed the part above the tower "the most beautiful wooden spire in New England" (church pamphlet). In 1946 it was found to be in such parlous structural condition that it had to be completely rebuilt.

The interior is typical of the Federal period with a long aisle, full-length galleries, and prominent pulpit. The pulpit is indeed magisterial in the overall and exemplary in detail. Note the delicacy of design in the facing of the panels with their swags, urns, triglyphs, and metopes. Add to this the scale of the overall framing and the precision of the Palladian window (curtained) and one encounters possibly the finest pulpit in New England. (If only the glare of the side windows could be toned down.) The paneling of the gallery, which repeats the pew spacing, should also be noted.

In spite of the importance of the church, its designer is unknown. Timothy Palmer is mentioned by some but he was basically a master carpenter, while church records show that the famous Samuel McIntire was paid for the carving. He might well have contributed more of his estimable expertise.

Note the Parish Hall of 1873 adjacent at right.

53

MEETINGHOUSE [1793]

Hancock Shaker Village
US 20
Pittsfield (Hancock); 5 miles/8 km
west of Pittsfield (Hancock not on
many tourist maps)

The focus of this book is religious architecture and it only peripherally touches on religion itself. It is, however, important in discussing Hancock Shaker Village to sketch briefly the Shakers themselves, particularly their differences from the Quakers with whom they are often confused. (See also the Shaker community at Sabbathday Lake, Maine; 32.) Whereas there are similarities between them, stemming in part from their rejection of creedal religion and their "trembling" when confronted with the word of God, the Shakers are celibate, hold property in common, and live in "Withdrawn" communities. Moreover, their correct title is the United Society of Believers in Christ's Second Appearing. The Quakers—from whom the Shakers sprang, and who are more properly known as the Religious Society of Friends ("Quaker" is a late seventeenth-century eponym)—marry, own property individually, and determinedly preach that "there is that of God in every human being" worldwide. For this latter practice they were co-awarded the Nobel Peace Prize in 1947.

In architecture both Shakers and Quakers are noted for their basically simple setting for worship with separate entries for men and women. The Shaker meetinghouses are externally marked by a characteristic gambrel (i.e., double angle) roof and within by an unobstructed ground floor for ritual dancing. Secular Shaker buildings are routine. As the Shakers were celibate, their membership was by conversion and adoption; however, there are only a handful of members remaining and the Shaker legacy now lives only in its heritage of buildings and the marvelously simple yet strangely sophisticated Shaker furniture and artifacts. In creating these, "beauty" was frowned upon—not necessarily the results.

The Meeting House now at Hancock originated in the northeastern Massachusetts town of Shirley during 1793. Dismantled in 1938, it was moved to this site in 1962 as one of the key buildings of the Shaker Village. The gambrel roof with dormers immediately proclaims the "standard" Shaker patterns as do the two entrances, one for sisters and the other for brethren. Note that there are separate doors for elders and eldresses on the side. The ground floor is free of supports or partitions to provide, as mentioned, unencumbered space for the famous Shaker dance ceremonies, the benches along the sides forming the only furniture. The second floor contains living quarters for two eldresses at one end and two elders at the other, the four being in charge of the community. The center rooms form offices shared by these leaders, each of whom had equal authority. Incidentally, the Shakers at the peak of their calling, just before the Civil War, reputedly never numbered more than 6,000 souls throughout their eighteen societies; there were about 300 at Hancock.

Also be sure to see the rest of the village-museum's seventeen buildings, especially the magnificent round stone barn of 1826, superbly restored in 1968. It is one of the great examples of American vernacular architecture.

54

FIRST UNIVERSALIST CHURCH
[1851]

236 Commercial Street
Provincetown

Benjamin Hallet, masterbuilder

Although outrageously hemmed in on a tiny site, the geometric trimness of the facade of this church enables it to hold its own against commercial shouldering. The contrast of the very narrow clapboards with bold pilasters and the triangle of the starkly plain pediment set a note of positiveness which is accented by the squared-away door and windows and their rectangular repetition above. On top rises a keen-edged tower with unusual banded pilasters, square belfry with inset Ionic columns, and octagonal lantern crowned by a copper-covered cupola—an ambitious lot.

The auditorium, on the second floor, is only of routine architecture but it boasts some of the most extraordinary *trompe l'oeil* paintings that one will see. They cover much of the ceiling, the pilasters, and panels on the walls, and there is a marvelous fool-the-eye exedra behind the pulpit. These "illusionistic" paintings—to use the description in the National Register of Historic Places—were the work of a young German artist named Carl Wendte. Very fresh. Although church records do not indicate a specific architect (Asher Benjamin's books are mentioned) the National Register says that the little-known Benjamin Hallet designed the church.

Rarely has a city's natural resource been so handsomely proclaimed as the famous granite of Quincy in this church by Alexander Parris. This crystalline quartz, feldspar, and mica rock girds the church's walls and bravely shoulders its 25-foot/7.6-m high Doric portico of Greek Revival ancestry. Moreover, most of the granite was a present from a Quincy local, President John Adams. Architect Parris was an early apostle of the Greek Revival movement which once shaped government buildings, banks, churches, and even left its mark on farmhouses in the 1820s and '30s. In the First Parish Church he created one of its most vigorous expressions. There is, of course, some question as to whether a Greek temple form is appropriate for a Christian church but let us here rejoice in the result. Under the portico note the slight height increase of the center door, lessening rigidity. Above the portico sits an authoritative square tower with inset clocks, its stone cubic form crowned by an airy wooden tempietto with dome (rebuilt in 1964).

The squarish interior is dominated by a remarkable ceiling approximately 70 feet/21 m in diameter. Its slightly domed form radiates deeply incised panels with rosettes in three rows from its inset floral center, the edge framed by a row of eighteen inset lotus blossoms. The galleries on the two sides are boldly supported by only one column. A monumental mahogany pulpit, flanked by two unusual marble plaques (to John Quincy and Francis Adams), and framed by doors and smaller panels under the galleries, fill the chancel wall. John Adams, his son John Quincy Adams and their wives are buried in the crypt.

On leaving note the 1844 Town Hall directly opposite.

55

UNITED FIRST PARISH CHURCH [1828]

1306 Hancock Street at Washington Quincy

Alexander Parris, architect

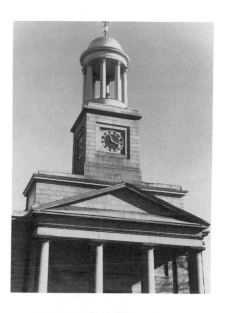

56

SOUTH CONGREGATIONAL
CHURCH [1875]

Maple and High Streets
Springfield

William C. Potter, architect

William Potter was an outstanding architect of an oft-preposterous era in the last half of the nineteenth century in which High Victorian Gothic encouraged a stylistic unshackling rarely seen in architecture of any period. (The heady Victorian Gothic should not be confused with the sedate Gothic Revival, which generally sought an authentic interpretation of medieval inspiration.) South Congregational's very original 120-foot/ 37-m tower dominates the exterior, especially from the curved uphill Maple Street approach, its wedge-shaped, multi-hued, shingled capping sitting with aplomb upon its rough red sandstone base, itself enlivened with bands of yellow Ohio sandstone. Note that horizontal bands of light-colored stone can be seen on all sides of the church "relieving" the dark stone walls. The High Street side calls on a rose window 26 feet/8 m in diameter in a gabled end for lateral emphasis, its circle repeated in a small window in the tower. A second gable adds to the vibration of angles on this side.

Although the exterior carries a somber reticence, the interior is alive in its integral treatment of the pulpit and organ and in the outreach of the wood trusswork. The organ sits in a niche behind the pulpit and forms a unity of design with it, the wainscoting of pulpit emphasized by the careful arrangement of organ pipes. The spidery tensions and compressions of the complicated trusswork which supports the roof are as dynamic visually as they are sound functionally. The 800-seat cross-shaped auditorium measures 91 feet/ 28 m by 71 feet/21.6 m.

"The carving in stone is one of the interesting features of the exterior—rosettes, ancient monograms, a sheaf of wheat, a cluster of grapes, or something of the kind, is worked into the gables everywhere, while the capitals of the pillars are some of them exquisitely carved, and all represent something in nature" (*The Congregational Quarterly*, July 1875). Hail an apotheosis, farewell to an era.

57

CONGREGATION BETH EL [1953/1968]

979 Dickinson Street
Springfield

Percival Goodman, architect

Temple Beth El is one of the great contemporary synagogues in the United States. In an era with "no distinctive style of architecture of Jewish houses of worship" (*Re-Dedication Journal,* Temple Beth El, 12 May 1968), Percy Goodman—who has designed "some fifty religious edifices"—has brought forth not only a distinctive building but one of the great fusions of religious architecture and art, a collaboration which in the 1950s was regarded warily by all. Ibram Lassaw, Adolph Gottlieb, Robert Motherwell—and others after them—were called on to give what might be termed a spiritual lift to earth-bound bricks. Lassaw's 28-foot/8.5-m bronze "Pillar of Fire," attached to the outside "prow" of the nave, gives electric vitality to the low-scaled facade; Gottlieb's woven curtain valence, brilliant with ritualistic symbols, brings color to the sanctuary; Motherwell's 18-foot/5.5-m tapestry decorates the small synagogue.

The original temple burned to the ground in 1965; however it was rebuilt three years later basically to the original design but with a larger worship room (now 674 seats) and more ancillary services. Joyfully, the new is even more impressive than photographs show of the old. The spacious 1968 auditorium is framed by substantial concrete bents angled upward to produce a dramatic, tent-like roof with a monitor through which the sun can pour over the sanctuary. A band of windows on either side provides the chief source of daylight. The rear walls can be opened via folding panels for expansion on High Holy Days. The angles of the low wall defining the bema (platform for clergy and dignitaries) are very effective in building a spatial climax to the *aron kodesh* (housing) for the Ark. The Ark valence and curtain in front of the Ark were designed by Efram Weitzman; the menorah, at left, by Lassaw. The wood grille of the organ, which stands against the rear wall, should be noticed as should the three slit windows on either side with stripes of orange and yellow glass. Throughout the temple there are other appropriate works of art. In all, Beth El represents a brilliant symbiosis of architect and artists working together from inception.

BAPTIST MEETINGHOUSE [1832]

Old Sturbridge Village
Southwest junction of Mass
   Turnpike and IS 86
Sturbridge

Old Sturbridge Village comprises a
revelatory collection of original
buildings brought here from various
parts of New England and laid out
to recreate a regional village of the
1830s. Thirty-eight period buildings,
mostly from the early nineteenth
century and ranging from a manor
house to a blacksmith's shop, will be
found, including a variety of dwell-
ings, two houses of worship, and
support facilities, all laid out with
the Village Green as nexus. The
Baptist Meetinghouse and the nearby
Friends Meetinghouse are both basic,
homely houses of worship of little
architectural distinction; however,
they play cohesive roles in the overall community development.

The Baptist Church, built in 1832,
came from nearby Sturbridge and, as
can be seen, forms the well-proportioned nodal point of the village, anchoring the Green. Situated on a
slight but strategic rise, its four columns, pediment, and steeple—basically Greek Revival—form a
constant reminder to the villagers of
the daily role of religion in their
lives. The details of the exterior are
simple, while the interior is almost
barren except for the yellowish
walls, the light blue ceiling, and
three surprisingly graceful chandeliers. When built, town meetings
also took place here; today there is in
summer a vesper service every Sunday afternoon.

The Quaker Meetinghouse, built
in 1796, was moved here from Bol-
ton, Massachusetts. Though utterly
plain without, the spaces within are
intriguing with galleries on three
sides impinging on the main floor.
Inside the projected vestibule there
are separate doors for men and
women.

Set back from the road, beautifully landscaped, artfully scaled, this synagogue is a complimentary component of its residential neighborhood. The invitation to enter is quietly there, the stages of enclosure gradual. The entrance to the temple is via a garden court as spatial intermedium, the wing of a previously existing unit framing the north side.

The worship room is a modified hexagon in shape—recalling the Star of David—and is upheld by six structural bents producing an extremely tidy interior. (From the exterior, the hexagon provides a "symbolic climax" to the massing.) The upper part of the six walls is almost completely filled with both clear and tinted glass shielded against interior glare (at times perhaps insufficiently) by vertical wood fins. (See Belluschi's similar, but later, Portsmouth Priory Chapel in Rhode Island [86]; also rewarding.) The sanctuary rests on a low brick platform whose pattern recalls that of the exterior walls. The problem of expansion for overflow congregations on High Holy Days—when a thousand or more attend—is solved by an auditorium which can be opened by means of folding doors directly off the entrance lobby and on axis with the chapel. The auditorium can also be used independently and is provided with stage and kitchen. Extensive administrative facilities and classrooms occupy the old wing and a lower level. Note the delicate "lantern" atop the hexagon with its Star of David. Very sympathetic.

59

TEMPLE ISRAEL [1955]

Humphrey Street, just east of
  Atlantic Avenue
Swampscott

Pietro Belluschi/Carl Koch, architects

60

INTERFAITH CENTER [1955]

Brandeis University
South Street just east of IS 95
Waltham

Harrison & Abramovitz, architects

The concept of grouping together chapels of America's three major religions—Protestant, Catholic, Jewish—has here been carried out with bold imagination. The three focus on a nondogmatic free-form pool (the Genetic waters?) with first-rate landscaping as backdrop. The Protestant Chapel, nearest the road, and the Catholic have the same orientation (northwest/southeast), with the Jewish chapel (shown here) at right angles, an informal path joining the three. The chapels are all built of the same grayish brick and each has the end facing the pool completely of glass, a visual cement as it were. It should be added that the chapels are carefully offset so that one does not see the other buildings from one's own. Capacity of the Jewish Chapel is approximately 100, while the other two accommodate 65–70. (Brandeis, although Jewish-founded, is a nonsectarian liberal arts university.) The chapels' overall shapes vary slightly and their interiors naturally reflect their particular liturgical demands; together they form a harmonious association. Inspired pansectarianism.

Wayland Unitarian is a large church that dominates its important crossroads site. Both church and the historic district which it borders are among the fringe benefits of downtown Boston, 15 miles/24 km to the east. The projected front of the church is unusual in having three equal-size doors with half-round fanlights and three slightly narrower round-headed windows above, the one in the center being Palladian. Stretched Doric pilasters divide the front into three flat bays, the whole topped by a pediment with an arced window the width of the Palladian motif below. The tower rises between porch and gabled block of the church to be capped by well-scaled balustrade. An airy octagonal belfry rests comfortably on the tower, topped by a lantern with unusual pointed arches on its eight sides. An extended dome and an elaborate weather vane crown all.

In the 1850s the interior was divided into two floors and "Victorian" style furnishings and paint took over; even the pulpit was removed. In the 1890s, though the two floors remained, an "un-Victorianization" took place so that today the interior, though divided, is seemly. Recently refurbished, the church and its carriage shed are now in fine shape. The Massachusetts Historical Commission states that the church was "built by Andrews Palmer from Asher Benjamin design."

61

FIRST PARISH UNITARIAN
CHURCH [1815]

US 20 at MA 27
Wayland

Asher Benjamin, architect

62

ST. JAMES THE FISHERMAN [1958]

Just west of US 6, north of Gulf
    Station
Wellfleet

Olav Hammarstrom, architect

An engaging summer chapel for
Episcopalians (and others) on the
midriff of Cape Cod. Topping a
knoll and engulfed by pine trees, the
simple stained-spruce chapel rests totally at home in its rustic setting.
Informality and provision for the
possibility of congregational partici-
pation in the service were requested
of the architect in developing its design. The low square mass of the
church is capped by a shingle-clad
elongated pyramid stalked above the
nave to form an airy bell tower. Beneath its single bell a square skylight
made of twenty-five plastic domes
pours down a flood of daylight—the
church's main source of illumination—onto the altar directly underneath. Auxiliary illumination and
ventilation come from an unusual
band of floor-level windows around
the periphery of the building. The
bright focus on the altar is further
intensified by the structure of the
belfry, whose eight wooden beams
frame the octagonal sanctuary as
they rise through the ceiling. The
pews are grouped in four banks on
the diagonal of the square plan, providing maximum closeness to the altar. A longitudinal annex for
administrative and related facilities
stands adjacent. Ingratiating.

63

WEST PARISH MEETINGHOUSE
[1719]

Mid-Cape Highway and MA 149
(south of 6A)
West Barnstable

One of the great early meeting-houses and, as the brochure states, "the oldest Congregational Church in the United States and the oldest public building on Cape Cod." Its location on a well-treed point of land gives it prominence while the land around gives it history: the whole Barnstable area is rich in tales of the sea and its clipper ships.

The squarish meetinghouse had, like many, a turbulent background, being cut in half and extended 18 feet/5.5 m only four years after its completion. A bell tower was added at this time, topped by a splendid weathercock, and a ceiling was installed to cut heat loss. By 1852, town meetings were no longer being held there and the church was in need of substantial repairs. The whole building was then reinforced, a new bell tower with spire erected, and the interior remodeled "to the neo-classic style characteristic of the mid-1800s" so that "nothing of the old Meetinghouse was visible" (church bulletin). One hundred years later a total restoration of the building was begun (finished in 1956), taking it back to its 1717–19 condition (without the 18-foot/5.5-m extension), removing the ceiling, replacing the bell tower, and otherwise authentically celebrating a marvelous ancient structure. The interior today is one of the finest, its wineglass pulpit rises properly paneled opposite the entry, the spindle-topped box pews establish their grid, and the now fully exposed structural truss-work adds visual pleasure. The results are a superb tribute to all who made the restoration possible.

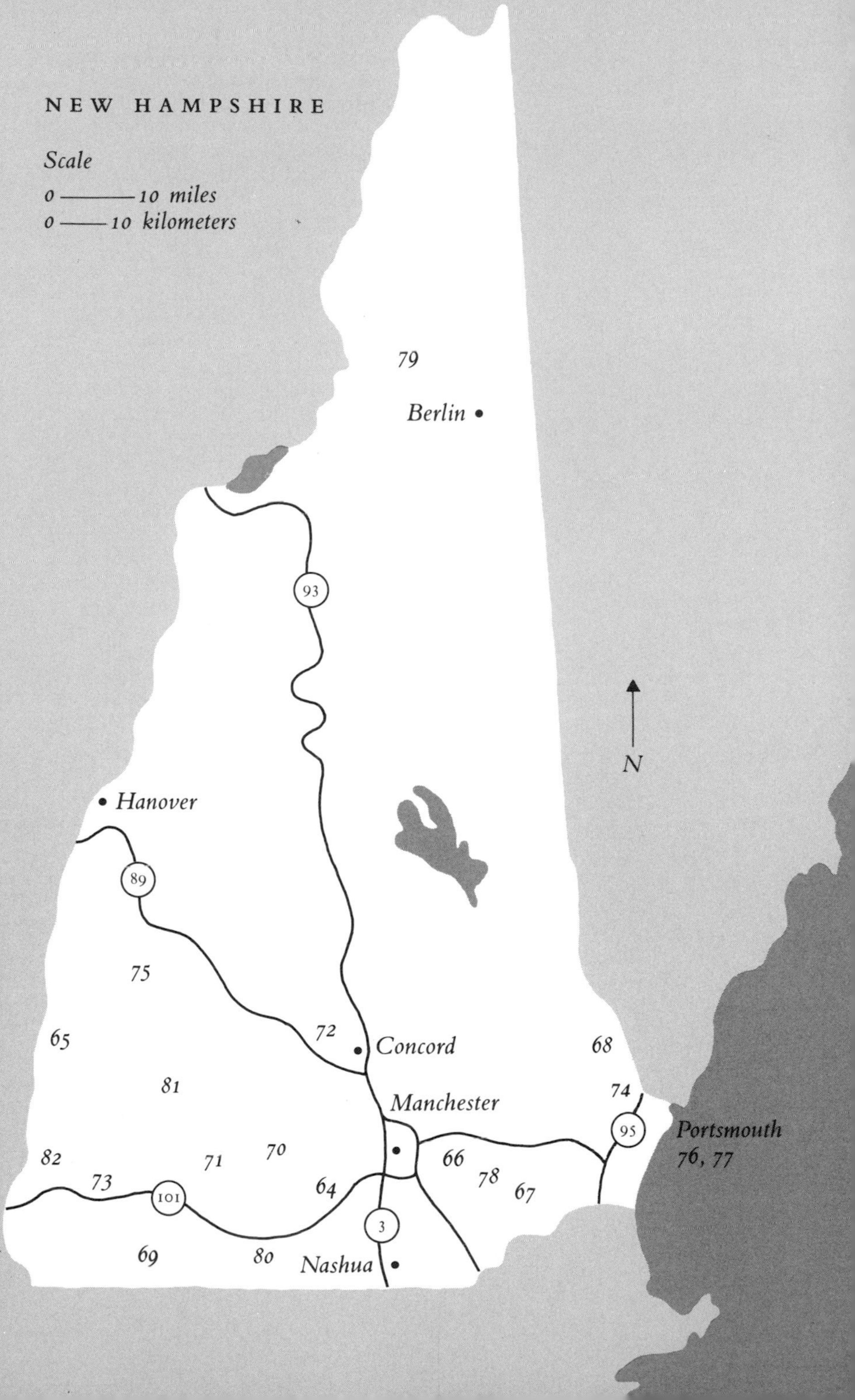

NEW HAMPSHIRE

Scale

0 ——— 10 miles
0 ——— 10 kilometers

79

Berlin •

93

• Hanover

89

75

65

81

72

65

Concord •

68

Manchester

74

82

71

70

66

78

67

95

73

101

64

Portsmouth
76, 77

69

80

Nashua •

3

N

THE CONGREGATIONAL CHURCH
[1774/1836] AND COMMON

Town Common
Amherst

The village of Amherst is centered on one of the most civilized commons to be seen. Of relaxed shape, it offers visual delight to all who pass by, while within its ample grounds it provides child space for mothers and benches and shade for the weary. A Civil War Memorial surveys all from the south edge. The church itself once occupied the Common but was moved across the street in 1836 when the Congregational Church and Society bought the property. It forms the dominant element of the square, being strategically placed near an intersection and embraced by trees. Dedicated in 1774, the 40 foot/12 m by 70 foot/21 m church underwent a drastic transformation when moved: it was jacked up and a lower floor inserted, while the entry which had been on the long side—as was typical of eighteenth-century meetinghouses—was closed and access provided by the present three doors in the gable end. A tower (with overscaled clocks) rises directly behind the pediment, crowned by octagonal belfry, blind belfry, and spire. The whole facade is good. The second-floor worship room is pleasant but not outstanding. Remodeled several times, it was completely rehabilitated in 1978. The church, its relation to the Common, and Amherst's overall ambiance make a rewarding excursion. The National Register lists it as the Amherst Village Historic District.

65

ST. LUKE'S EPISCOPAL CHURCH
[1863/1869]

Main Street/NH 12
Charlestown

Richard Upjohn, architect

A quaint, little-known wooden church by the famous English-born Upjohn (Trinity Church, New York, etc.), one with an almost Scandinavian vernacular in its tower and roof angles. If the exterior seems on the lively side it is because the original "reticent" church was cut in half six years after completion—to meet the great increase of congregation—and 22 feet/6.7 m, the transept, and the smartly profiled pivotal tower were added under the direction of the architect's son, R. M. Upjohn. Board and batten sheathe the exterior with one of the earlier polychrome slate roofs above. The nave is sedate and intimate, highlighted by the senior Upjohn's imaginative—and functional—wooden trusswork. The recessed hexagonal chancel, its altar moved forward in the early 1980s, gives focus to the interior. The memorial windows largely date from the 1880s.

An upland village church characterized by an interaction of sharply sliced forms. It measures 40 feet/12 m by 75 feet/23 m. The trim facade of Greek Revival influence is topped by a clean-cut pediment echoed in its center by a sharp triangular vent. The well-scaled square tower carries three black circular clocks, with louvered belfry above framed by thin pilasters and topped by a small pediment of its own. The spire juts heavenward but is cleverly turned at an angle of 45° to the church axis, the better to catch the sun. The whole facade and the steeple are of flush boarding while the sides are clapboarded. The worship room continues the basic simplicity of the outside with restrained but delicate detailing. It seats 300. What we see today, however, dates from the total remodeling of 1839 when the church "was turned around, the spire cut away, the interior altered" (church bulletin).

In the 1940s the First Baptist Church of Chester could no longer support a separate organization and yoked with the Congregational Church, the official name thereafter being the Congregational-Baptist Church of Chester.

As the National Register Nomination Form states, the church is "significant as one of the major examples of the Greek Revival in southeastern New Hampshire."

66

CONGREGATIONAL CHURCH
[1773/1839]

NH 102 and 121
Chester

67

MEETINGHOUSE [1760]

On NH 111A about 3.2 mi/5 km
   north of NH 111
Danville

This sharply gabled, almost primitive box of a meetinghouse epitomizes the rigorous housing for religion seen in much of eighteenth-century New England. Its pared shape, 37 feet/11 m by 49 feet/15 m, with scant eaves in front and back and none on ends, proclaims an ultimate reduction. The discreetly detailed white-painted main door—there are plainer side entries—punctuates the long side opposite the pulpit, while black-framed windows stir a dynamic counterpoint of contrasts in the facade. Note the graduated width of the clapboards.

The interior with the usual three-sided gallery is of sturdy simplicity—with heavily braced frame—enlivened by a towering pulpit with sounding board and spindle-topped pews. The off-white panels of the galleries are mostly original. The meetinghouse was roughly handled in the last century after its religious use phased out and its town hall functions moved to a new and more convenient location (1878). At one point the pews were taken out and the hall reputedly used for dancing. In 1911, however, the Old Meetinghouse Association was established to preserve the building, and in 1936 a local citizen gave funds for the return of the pews, which had been saved, and it has been proudly maintained since. It is a rare and little changed trophy of a past age. Be sure to visit the cemetery.

68

Off 141 Central Avenue
Dover

Withdrawn, almost domestic in scale, the Dover Meetinghouse's function is revealed only by its coupled front doors, one for sisters, the other for brethren, and both, it should be stressed, of strict equality. (The vestibule probably dates from the early 1800s.) The Quakers, more correctly the Religious Society of Friends, have no ordained clergy—though there are "elders"—and no formal liturgy. (They have, of course, a fully staffed religious organization.) Thus their houses of worship have no need for the axial "sanctuary" with altar and pulpit typical of other Christian churches. This building measures 50 feet/15 m by 37 feet/11 m.

The interior architectural response seen here has benches along the four walls with open space in the center for nonformalized "meetings for worship." These meetings, often characterized by silence and generally lasting an hour, are open to all who might participate and wish to proclaim communion between God and humankind. The long (north) wall opposite the entry contains the "facing bench" used by the elders. Because art and architecture (as well as music) were considered "frivolous" by Quakers until well into the twentieth century, unpretentiousness, both outside and in, marked their meetinghouses. It is seen here in this well-maintained building, the last surviving eighteenth-century example in New Hampshire, of the dozen or so originally in the state.

The minute village of Fitzwilliam, peacefully off the main highway, focuses on a small common embellished by a war memorial and two churches of which the more handsome is this meeting house, also known as Trinity Baptist-Town Hall. When organized religious services ceased in the 1860s, town functions occupied the whole building and it was remodeled into two floors, overall measurement being 58 feet/18 m wide by 66 feet/20 m long. The interiors thus are no longer of architectural interest. However, the exterior is one of Elias Carter's finest, its tower, belfry, cupola, and spire being notable—and almost an exact duplicate of his Federated Church in Templeton, Massachusetts. Carter, born in Massachusetts, was very active in New England church architecture, his use of two well-separated pairs of Ionic columns at entry becoming almost a trademark. Also seen in other examples of his work is a fondness for using an arched open belfry atop a square tower, with two octagonal, almost elaborate stages above, and spire atop.

Although the National Register Nomination Form does not list an architect for the building, Edmund W. Sinnott's excellent *Meeting House and Church in Early New England* (McGraw-Hill, 1963) lists it under Elias Carter's works.

69

FITZWILLIAM MEETINGHOUSE
[1817]

Just west of NH 12 on NH 119
Fitzwilliam

Elias Carter, architect

70

THE OLD MEETINGHOUSE [1801]

NH 47 and 116
Francestown

The upland crossroads hamlet of Francestown "has a serene and unspoiled quality. It is unusually rich in domestic and ecclesiastical architecture dating from the 1780's to the 1830's" (from Bryant F. Tolles, Jr.'s wonderfully comprehensive guide *New Hampshire Architecture*). The First Church, though altered through the years, gives a graceful focus to a group of nineteenth-century structures typical of New England village vernacular. The church itself, as Tolles points out, was "thoroughly remodeled" in 1834, when the excellent Greek Revival details and steeple were added. (The steeple was rebuilt in 1855 when a new and heavier bell was installed.) Note that while the three doors are identical (as are the windows), the outer two are not centered in their bay, but "cluster" toward the middle to produce livelier proportions. Ionic pilasters and good entablature add to this distinguished facade. The interior is of less interest. The church was extensively renovated and spruced up in 1953. It faces the Town Hall (1847) and Grange with an extensive carriage shed alongside. In 1987 its title was transferred from the Unitarian Church to the Old Meetinghouse of Francestown, Inc.

Driving north on NH 47 one will see a good collection of early nineteenth-century houses, mostly of Federal inspiration.

The remote and elevated village of Hancock offers the visitor a relaxed, even detached vignette of semirural highland New England. Moreover, its meetinghouse/town hall is one of Carter's more interesting. (See also his work at Fitzwilliam [69] and influence at Newport [75].) The boldly projected front at Hancock is dominated by three closely aligned dark front doors—expressing the Trinity—with the usual Palladian window above, here flanked by curiously overscaled rectangular windows. Coupled pilasters (instead of the columns seen at Fitzwilliam) terminate the front and are repeated on the edges of the facade. Over this rises Carter's tower and steeple, the almost identical design of which can be seen in the other two churches mentioned above: square belfry, displaying bold round-headed openings, set inside a balustrade with pinnacles on the corners, and topped by a two-stage octagonal tower elaborately attended to. (The upper "window" is merely paint: note that it repeats the oval in the pediment). Spire and bright weather vane crown all. The bell, incidentally, was made in Paul Revere's factory in 1820, two years after his death.

In 1851 the meetinghouse was moved from its first site across the green to its present location and an upper floor put in for religious services, town functions occupying the lower. Renovations were carried out in 1966 but the interiors are not distinguished. Overall upkeep has been excellent. Note the curve of the 1895 carriage shed along the back: it measures almost 180 feet/55 m long.

The entire main street of Hancock is rewarding, especially the nearby Congregational Vestry of 1836.

71

CONGREGATIONAL CHURCH [1820] AND VILLAGE

Village Green (NH 127/137) Hancock

Elias Carter, architect

72

ST. ANDREW'S EPISCOPAL
CHURCH [1828]

NH 9 and 202
Hopkinton

John Leach, architect

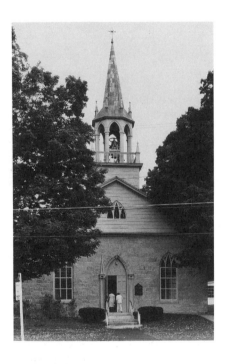

A piquant "gothick" village church
in a very seemly village. Its thick
gray ashlar walls are of locally quar-
ried granite—which once stopped a
devastating town fire from spreading
(1927)—with the tops of front door
and windows carefully pointed in
the approved Gothic fashion. The
pointed arch motif is repeated,
somewhat unsatisfactorily, in the
wood pediment above. The original
church tower was square but problems with leakage caused its removal
in 1919; it was not until 1920 that
the present sympathetic belfry and
spire were added. The new tower's
design was by the firm of Cram &
Ferguson of Boston. (Ralph Adams
Cram, 1863–1942, probably the most
famous church architect of the early
twentieth century, was born in
Hampton Falls, New Hampshire.)
The belfry's lightness is accented by
its pointed arches, and its octagonal
form is topped by a spire which has
an imaginative "bent" spruced by
eight small crockets.

The interior of the church, though
not brilliant architecturally, is very
much a member of the well-known
family of nineteenth-century "gothick" Episcopal churches—shades of
Pugin and Ruskin—complete with
Victorian stained glass (here dating
from the 1890s). The chancel has
been twice remodeled, but the box
pews were left intact.

Henri Focillon (1881–1943), the great French art historian, proposed that the development of all art evolved in three basic stages—experimental, classic, and baroque. One can see this in the evolution of the work of most artists, and in architecture one can trace the progress from, say, archaic Greek temples to the Parthenon. Thus it was with the evolutionary design of this church in southwest New Hampshire, which began as a meetinghouse in 1786, moved to its present site on the Common in 1829, and in the 1860s metamorphosed into the 60 by 90 foot/18 by 27 m structure we see today. It is probably the most "baroque" church of the nineteenth century in New England, a final fillip being given the spire following the destruction of the older one by the 1938 hurricane. It tops out at 130 feet/40 m. The United Church (a merger of the First Congregational with the Court Street Congregational) rejoices in a richness of elements that are staggering if at times strangely mixed up (as with the round-headed coupled windows of Italian Romanesque derivation combined with the rich Corinthian columns and pilasters of the front.) The tower and spire spring 152 feet/46 m heavenward with a panache of daring exuberance. The interior, while competent, lacks the verve of the facade. It had to.

73

UNITED CHURCH OF CHRST
[1786–1861]

23 Central Square
Keene

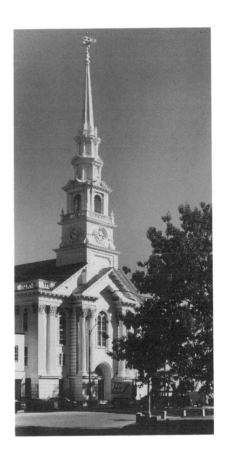

74

TOWN CHURCH CONGREGATIONAL
[1712]

Exit 4 south from Spaulding
    Turnpike about 1.5 mi/2.4 km
    west; 316 Nimble Hill Road
Newington

From the framed notice in front of
the church: "Believed to be the oldest in continual use in the nation
built in 1712 from taxes levied on
polls and estates of inhabitants. (Author's note: it is the oldest Congregational church in continuous use.
Old Ship in Hingham, Massachusetts
[48] has been active since 1681.)
Originally a spire, twice struck by
lightning, left as is. Bell given to
people of Newington from Newington, England. When eventually
cracked, bell hauled by oxcart to
Boston and recast by P. Revere 1810.

"Present entrance was private entry to pew of settlement's wealthiest
citizen, Col. John Downing member
of Royal Governor's Council. He
was also granted liberty for a window—and later other more affluent
members also got windows. Many
of present windows thus installed.
Main entrance was on South Side.
Gallery for negro slaves and inden-
tured servants surrounded three
sides. All box pews on ground floor
privately owned and handed down
from generation to generation as
were carriage sheds at rear."

This chubby, oft-changed church
exhibits a fine play of geometry, the
half-round tops of its door, windows, and belfry counterpointing the
box of the nave and the triangles of
the pediments. Major changes, almost a rebuilding, took place in
1835. The interior is a basically
square room of minimum elabora-
tion, the box pews forming the major visual interest.

An imposing Federal Style church whose brick walls with recessed arched panels, support an ambitious tower. The body of the church with projected front and its carefully proportioned doors and windows is excellent, the springing of its discreet arches marked by a terse band of white stone and dark wood shutters. The rhythm here is first-rate, the arches of the walls echoed by the lunettes over the three doors. The wooden tower and its four stages above are also well designed but to this eye overscaled. The design of the tower brings out an interesting point of authorship because its basic divisions and their treatment can be clearly seen in several churches by Elias Carter: his church at Fitzwilliam (69) on the south edge of the state, dating from 1818, and his church at Hancock (71), 13 miles/ 21 km to the south of Newport, dating from 1820. Yet the church manual of 1887 states that "John Leach, a noted builder, framed it"—no mention of Carter. All three churches have a square tower with arched and pilastered open belfry above, octagonal lantern, and richly detailed stage and cupola. It would seem that Leach had taken his sketch pad with him on his travels—a not unknown proclivity of architects—plus using the several "handbooks" that were available.

The interior of South Congregational is marked by a cream-colored cheerfulness and by a veritable parade of Ionic columns and pilasters. The ceiling forms a shallow longitudinal dome which is repeated over the inset sanctuary, the whole distinguished by expert detailing. It was remodeled in 1853, "completely modernized" in 1868, the "colored glass" windows were installed in 1877, and the whole handsomely restored in 1983. The addition at rear dates from 1984.

Note: the Unitarian Church (1826) at Peterborough on NH 101 is similar in basic form to this in Newport, but the interior is not as satisfactory.

75

SOUTH CONGREGATIONAL CHURCH [1823]

NH 10, south of intersection with NH 11
Newport

76

ST. JOHN'S EPISCOPAL CHURCH
[1808]

101 Chapel Street
Portsmouth

Alexander Parris, architect

Though topping a hill, St. John's urban presence today is not felicitous, being closely pressed by its neighbors and rising abruptly from a busy street. Its tower and octagonal lantern, however, should be noted, the latter being particularly handsome. But if the Federal-influenced exterior with its arched panel walls and suppressed ornament is not exceptional, the interior represents another perspective of architectural design altogether. Instead of simplicity we find an outburst of creative elements, the best of them coordinated, the others an accumulation. The densely occupied chancel represents such a contrast to those in most of the churches in this book that it should be experienced to complete the panoply of the possible. In addition the ceiling and walls delight in a *trompe l'oeil* canopy that has few equals. This fool-the-eye "shadow" painting envelops the worshiper to create a startling ambiance. It was carried out in 1848 by Daniel M. Shepard and carefully restored in 1951. "Although skillfully done, there are widely varying views as to whether the painting adds or detracts from the overall" (Robert E. McLaughlin, *On Church Hill,* 1982). The church—the first brick one in the state—measures 61 feet/19 m wide by 88 feet/27 m long.

A number of internal changes occurred in the late nineteenth century: box pews were replaced by slip pews (1867), clear windows gave way to stained glass (1885–), the original pulpit moved from center to side, and "a series of memorial tablets of varying styles and dates" added. Unique.

77

UNITARIAN UNIVERSALIST
CHURCH [1826]

292 State Street
Portsmouth

Alexander Parris, architect

The Piscataqua River's safe harbor-
age brought settlers to this region as
early as 1623. In time the village of
Portsmouth flourished on the banks
of what is New Hampshire's only
seaport, prospering via timber, ship-
building and fishing. A splendid heritage of architecture resulted from
Colonial days to the mid nineteenth
century; indeed, the city (now some
30,000 in population) has one of the
most notable collections of historic
houses in the United States. When
urban "renewal" (often urban destruction) threatened to wipe out
much of Portsmouth's distinguished
physical past, concerned citizens
formed in 1958 the Strawbery Banke
Restoration to preserve the city's historic core. Their efforts were brilliantly successful and Strawbery
Banke—the town's genial original
name—should be seen by all scout-
ing for churches in New England.

Among the notable examples is this somewhat formidable church with 2-foot/1.6 m-thick dressed granite walls and bold portico. It measures 66 feet/20 m wide by 92 feet/28 m long. The spireless façade is of Greek Revival design—one of the earlier—and at the dedication of the now restored church (1987) the minister said, "This building was conceived as an expression of the new Unitarian religious outlook. It was to represent a Greek forum where the quest for truth is pursued unfettered and the method of organization was to be wholly democratic—with no vestige whatever of creedal or clerical authoritarianism."

The slightly vaulted, coffered interior, having no side galleries, delivers an open unitary space well lit by its tall windows. However, it was reputedly considered "spiritless" in the mid nineteenth century and in 1858 it underwent a major transformation into "the Italian Style," including a 17-foot/5 m extension. After a century of hesitancies and renovations a complete interior restoration was carried out in 1987. The dominant feature is a recessed chancel framed by Corinthian pilasters with an extraordinary broken scroll pediment above and a rich entablature reaching out on either side. Framing the chancel are prominent horseshoe-shaped panels, one containing the Lord's Prayer and the other the Ten Commandments. Not incidentally, the church's sturdy granite walls were erected by a mastermason named Jonathan Folsom who had his apprenticeship building the stone docks at the Portsmouth Navy Yard. Although no signed plan by Parris has been found, most historians consider him the architect.

The church, originally Unitarian, merged with the Universalist Church and Society in 1947.

78

MEETINGHOUSE [1774]

Fremont Road off NH 111A
Sandown

The meetinghouse in Sandown is one of the few that have survived unchanged through the years. Boxy and capped by an unpunctured statement of a roof with tightly gabled eaves, the basic simplicity of the white clapboard exterior is perked by a well-detailed entry (aligned with window heads) and a neatly denticulated cornice. The two side entries resemble the double door in the long front facing the pulpit but are single width.

The unspoiled interior, measuring 50 feet/15 m wide by 44 feet/13 m deep, offers a setting for religion that is visually rigorous and physically demanding (being heatless). The towering paneled pulpit with the usual window behind (here curtained), the box pews, and the gallery on three sides are all precisely as built over 200 years ago. Note the marbleizing around the pulpit and on the columns upholding the balcony. All other wood is natural finish. The hardware is, of course, handwrought. Used by the Congregational Society only until 1834, town meetings were continued in the building until 1929. As a consequence it has been excellently maintained, a fact which makes it of great value in the study of eighteenth-century construction. Sandown is one of the great touchstones of our inheritance: "one of the finest in America" (Harold Wickliffe Rose, *The Colonial Houses of Worship in America,* Hastings House, 1963). Today it is carefully watched over by the Old Meeting House Historical Association.

79

UNION CHURCH [1853] AND
COVERED BRIDGE [ca. 1852]

NH 110
Stark

Architectural elegance will not be found in this northern New Hampshire church, but it forms such an evocative image with the adjacent—and contemporary—covered bridge that in many ways it is a syllabus of New England. The church exterior is tidy but the plastered interior is of little interest. As the only church in the tiny village of Stark, it plays an active role in the community, and is carefully maintained by the Pew Owners' Association. Simple Greek Revival details surround the entries while hesitant "Gothic" pinnacles are found on the tower. It measures 36 feet/11 m wide by 46 feet/14 m deep.

The bridge, incidentally, is of the Paddleford truss type with a sufficient roof overhang to shelter the pedestrian walks on either side. However bridges were covered primarily to protect their structural framing from the weather.

Temple is a tiny village in the southern hills of the state and though this religio-civic grouping is not significant as a collection of buildings, it provides a picturesque insight into the socio-urban development of scores of similar New England towns. Moreover, the camaraderie of their gables determinedly surveying the landscaped park in front and the distant hills is also rewarding. The building on the left, with strong pediment and modified Greek Revival details, is the First Congregational Church (1842). Its simple interior has been recently spruced up. Close by is the small Congregational Chapel of 1887 with addition of 1951. Beyond, the former Universalist Church (1842) crowns the rise and now serves as town hall and grange. The brick Mansfield Memorial Library (1890) ends the parade. No sophistication will be found, but the fraternal centricity of these buildings, their statement of white-painted wood with dark windows, the positive searching of their south-facing gables, and their respectful spacing encapsulate much of the small New England village of the early nineteenth century.

81

CHURCH AND CIVIC GROUP
[1780s–1880s]

NH 31
Washington

The upland hamlet of Washington, incorporated in 1776, boasts one of the most engaging collections of white clapboard public buildings to be seen in New England. Moreover the buildings are set back from the road with a hillside of white pines as backdrop, small park with the proper monument (1867) in front, and the Monadnock Mountains vanishing in the distance. None of the three buildings in this cluster is architecturally distinguished but their spatial comradeship and identity of material generate a comely, almost wistful grouping. The Congregational Church (to left in photograph) was built in 1840: it is spartan both outside and in except for a bravely pinnacled two-stage tower. It measures 40 feet/12 m wide by 50 feet/15 m long. The central building, the school, dates from 1883, and the Town Hall from 1787. The latter served both secular and religious needs until the church was built, its dual function accented by the addition of a competent tower and spire in 1820, probably inspired by Asher Benjamin's *The Country Builder's Assistant* of 1797. Unspoiled delight.

82

PARK HILL CHURCH [1764/1824]

NH 63
Westmoreland

Park Hill Church impresses in spite of past tribulations: it was twice moved (1779 and 1824) and drastically altered the second time. It was settled on this commanding hilltop—only some 90 feet/27 m north of its first site—to have "a higher and more prominent location, and thus allowed the new (present) facade with its tower and portico to be seen to better advantage from the surrounding countryside" (National Register Nomination Form). The facade of the nearly square church is out of the ordinary in that its projected portico with rich pediment is upheld by widely spaced twin Tuscan columns, leaving the center surprisingly open and inviting. Three equal doors under a bold entablature cluster beneath with matching windows high above. Pairs of pilasters secure the edges. Above rises (a bit too high) the tower with the usual Palladian window. The tower is topped by a square belfry with round-headed windows flanked by paired pilasters, which are repeated at smaller scale in the octagonal lantern. The whole is finished off by dome and weather vane. Imaginative detailing with some Greek Revival touches are found throughout. The projected portico is similar to that of the Trinity Baptist Church in Fitzwilliam (1817; 69); the latter was designed by the well-known Elias Carter but there is no attribution of his hand at Park Hill.

Coinciding with the 1824 moving, church records show that 20 feet/6 m were added to the nave, and the present portico, tower, and steeple erected. In 1853 a second floor was inserted and the windows lengthened, the auditorium, as usual, occupying the upper level. The church interior is thus of secondary interest.

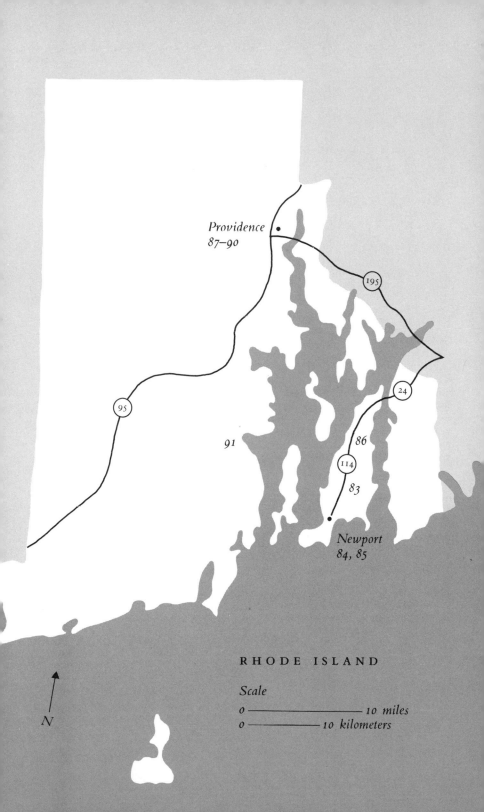

Providence
87–90

195

95

24

91

86

114

83

Newport
84, 85

N

RHODE ISLAND

Scale

0 ———————— 10 miles
0 ———————— 10 kilometers

83

CHURCH OF THE HOLY CROSS
[1845]

About 3 mi/4.8 km north of
    Newport, east side of RI 114
Middletown-Newport

Richard Upjohn, architect

This tiny, little-known Episcopal
chapel by Upjohn (see also his Grace
Church in Providence; 90) will delight visitors in the Newport area.
As mentioned in the descriptive
booklet available at the church, "It is
rustic in its exterior, and thus admi-
rably adapted to its isolated position
in the country: but so chaste in its
interior finish, and so perfect in its
proportion, that it is more imposing
in its religious impression and far
better adapted to its sacred use than
many buildings of far greater cost
and pretensions." The exterior is
covered with white-painted fishscale
shingles accented by gray trim. The
minute interior is indeed "perfect
in proportion" with only minor
changes through the years, the altar
and reredos dating from 1895. A
complete refurbishing took place in
1970 when a cellar was installed;
since then the church has been beautifully maintained. It should be
added that Upjohn was active in
Rhode Island for more than a de-
cade, designing both churches and
houses.

84

TRINITY CHURCH [1726]

141 Church Street at Spring
Newport

Richard Munday, architect

Richard Munday (ca. 1690–1739) reportedly started professional life in Newport as an innkeeper. However, he soon became a carpenter and, with apprenticeship, an architect sufficiently accomplished to design the impressive Trinity Church. (His most noted work is the nearby Colony House of 1739.) Trinity, as is generally pointed out, was largely based on Christ Church (Old North) in Boston, finished two years before Trinity in 1724, with Wren's and Gibbs's work in London as secondary inspiration. Trinity's flattery of Christ Church is immediately apparent on the exterior, for the wood belfry, lantern, and spire (the latter finished in 1741) atop each are virtually identical. (The body of Christ Church, incidentally, is of brick whereas Trinity is altogether of wood.) Another of the exterior pleasures of Trinity can be seen in its location at the top of a park which slopes down almost to the harbor. (Newport had one of the busiest harbors in the Colonies during the mid eighteenth century: shipping was its chief source of income and, it might be said, made the church possible.) Queen Elizabeth II dedicated the upper park in 1976 for the U.S. Bicentennial. The body of the exterior

of the church is noteworthy for its white beaded clapboards and its seriatim parade of round-headed windows.

The interior also recalls Old North, with similar galleries on either side given cadence by the super-imposed square columns which mark each bay, and by the bays' cross vaulting that extends from the windows to the nave. An exedra terminates the sanctuary of each church with a splendid wineglass pulpit in front, that at Trinity on center. In 1762 the building was cut in two and 30 feet/ 9 m added to its overall length. A restoration was effected in 1936— removing the garish nineteenth-century paint and stained glass—and the church was overhauled again in 1988. It is now sparkling. It is pleasant to note that real candles are still used in the chandeliers. The organ was reputedly tested by Handel before being shipped from England.

85

TOURO SYNAGOGUE [1763]

85 Touro Street at Division
Newport

Peter Harrison, architect

The National Register of Historic Places lists this synagogue not just as a building but as "Touro Synagogue National Historic Site," for, transcending its excellent architecture, it is a beacon of the religious freedom which was woefully absent from New England even well into the eighteenth century. Roger Williams (ca. 1603–83), who was banished from the Puritan Massachusetts Colony in 1635 because of his liberal views, established Rhode Island—one might say invented Rhode Island—as a land of religious freedom for all faiths, non-Puritan Christians and Jews. (He also established the Baptist Church in the Colonies.)

The Touro Synagogue, also called Temple Jeshuat Israel, was named for Isaac de Abraham Touro, a Sephardic "reader" who emigrated from Amsterdam in 1758 and revitalized Newport's small Jewish population. Today the house of worship which they erected is particularly dear to all Jews as being the oldest standing synagogue in the United States. It is, in addition, a masterpiece by Peter Harrison (1716–75). This extraordinarily talented man, who was a shipping magnate by profession and only an amateur architect, was born and educated in England, hence familiar with architectural fashions there, especially the work of William Kent and James Gibbs. He was also—relevant here—familiar with Bevis Marks, a Spanish-Portuguese synagogue built in London in 1701 and designed by a fellow Quaker, Joseph Avis. Lacking a pattern of building which characterizes most Christian churches, Jewish houses of worship through the years have taken a variety of architectural expressions. Harrison, who had finished his elegant and nearby Redwood Library of 1750, used some of the Palladian-inspired elements of that building in his Georgian Touro design.

The exterior of the synagogue, which is angled so that the Ark of the Covenant will face east, comprises a simple two-story box form with hipped roof, a parade of round-headed windows on both levels, belt course, and well-proportioned portico in front. (The gate and fence were designed by Isaiah Rogers in 1844.) The two-story interior, however, is probably the most sophisticated in the United States. Its space, which measures approximately 40 feet/12 m long by 30 feet/9 m wide, is compacted by the galleries on three sides, the top one for women and the lower for men, with benches along the sides. The galleries are supported by twelve Ionic columns (Corinthian above) representing the twelve tribes of Israel. An ornately enclosed pulpit for reading the Law occupies the center. Detailing throughout is elegant.

After the Revolution, Newport's fortunes declined drastically and most of the temple's congregation moved to New York City, leaving the synagogue closed for much of the nineteenth century. However, Isaac de Abraham Touro's sons left money in their wills for the support of the temple—giving it the popular name it now carries—and it has flourished ever since. One of the greats.

PORTSMOUTH PRIORY CHAPEL
[1961]

West off RI 144 via Cory's Lane
Portsmouth

Pietro Belluschi, architect

Pietro Belluschi for many years has designed some of our most distinguished houses of worship; this chapel is one of his masterpieces. Elevated on a low stone terrace and in plan an octagon on a circular base with an attached rectangular wing, its walls of native stone and redwood rise to frame the high wooden octagon of the nave. The slenderest of spires on top vanishes heavenward. The stone of the walls and the sympathy of the natural wood bind the chapel to its rural surroundings, while the stepped profile makes its scale an ingratiating neighbor to the school buildings. The seven stone panels, which alternate with wood to form the lower walls, are solid except at entry: they are bowed inward in plan both for strength and shadow play. Between them are panels of vertically expressed wood bowed outward. (Their vertical expression visually ties them to the upper part of the nave.) The tall wood octagon framing the center rises with precise geometry to be roofed with folded planes of copper topped by a short lantern and an impeccably perched spire.

The two-story interior consists of nave for 180 students and retrochoir for 60 Benedictine brothers. Its space is crowned by the upper part of the nave which is enclosed with alternating strips of wood and stained glass (by Henry Lee Willet). This glass, though subdued in color (mostly blues with touches of red) wraps a spirited mantle around the worship room. Over the high altar between nave and choir a tiny statue of Christ is suspended on scores of gold and silver wires that give brilliant focus to the altar as they reach out to knit the spaces together. This metallic veil by Richard Lippold is one of the finest works of religious art to be seen. George Nakashima was responsible for the design and carving of the stone altars, pews, and many interior details. They "all combine to make of the church at Portsmouth Priory another example of that buoyant revival of Benedictine vitality in the field of religious architecture in the United States" *(Liturgical Arts, February 1963).* On the periphery of the nave are six side altars for the monks to say daily Mass, with four more altars in the gallery. The front door was beautifully incised with ancient Roman lettering by Father Peter. Anderson, Beckwith & Haible were associate architects. Superb.

87

FIRST BAPTIST CHURCH [1775]

75 North Main Street between
    Waterman and Thomas
Providence

Joseph Brown, architect

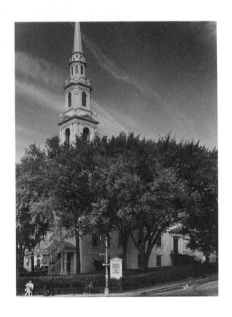

The Baptist Church in America was
founded in Providence in 1639 by
Roger Williams, the apostle for freedom of religion (which he termed
"soul liberty") in the Colonies. This,
the third church for its faith in that
town and the oldest Baptist Church
in America, is one of the most accomplished in New England. It
adapts professionally to its corner
site with its sharp change in level, its
tower and spire rank high aestheti-
cally, and its gabled box form with
rows of round-headed windows are
more than well proportioned. The
chief entry on Main Street has a classic Georgian portico supported by
two pairs of Tuscan columns topped
by rich entablature. Behind rises the
projected front with tower above,
prominent quoins and a Palladian
window marking the lower part,
with a belt course tying entry to the
block of the church. The 185-foot/
56-m steeple was taken almost in
toto from a plate in James Gibbs's
Book of Architecture published in London in 1728 but, as the church booklet points out, "one must not forget

that Joseph Brown chose and improved it with unerring taste." The booklet also shows how the spire was designed in telescoping sections, each hoisted up by windlass within the shell of the lower, no scaffolding being required.

The worship room, which because of grade fall-off is located on the second floor, measures 80 by 80 feet/24 by 24 m—a square plan was unusual for its day—and forms a cheerful space. It was built somewhat larger than its congregational needs to accommodate commencements at nearby Brown University. It seats 800 on the main floor and 600 in the gallery. The nave's two-story blocked columns, four on each side and two at entry, flair into vaulted bays which meld with the vault of the ceiling to develop interior liveliness. The crystal chandelier of Waterford glass dates from 1792. The gallery "once seated Indians, slaves, and freedmen." In 1846 the Palladian window back of the pulpit was plastered over but in 1884 its space was opened with an awkward extension to house a baptistery complete with stained-glass window. "Decorative painting" was applied to the ceiling. Fortunately, in 1957–58 the whole church was restored to its original design, enclosing the baptistery, and the interior was repainted in a sage green color instead of the white which had been applied in 1832. Funds for the restoration were given by John D. Rockefeller, Jr., who had taught Sunday school in the church when he was a student at Brown University. Joseph Brown, the architect, was a professor of mathematics.

88

BENEFICENT CONGREGATIONAL
CHURCH [1810/1836]

300 Weybosset Street at Chestnut
Providence

Barnard Eddy/James Bucklin, architects

The Beneficent Church is unique
outside and in. Its rectangular brick
form is surmounted by a paneled
parapet and topped by a shining
dome (restored in 1987) which rests
on a high octagonal plinth. Crowning the dome—locally known as
Round Top—is a copy of the Chor-
agic Monument of Lysicrates (335
B.C.) in Athens. A bold Greek Revival portico (1836) proclaims the
entry.

The almost overwhelming feature
of the interior is the multistepped
chancel (1857) with, seemingly, cascades of pews for choir and clergy,
the whole backed by an organ (1923)
of startling prominence to emphasize
the church's regard for music. The
nave itself forms a handsome space,
with extra-deep stepped galleries
supported by two-story fluted Ionic
columns, four per side.

The original church was designed
by the little-known Barnard Eddy
with, reputedly, "a dome influence"
via the Irish-born minister's nostalgia
for the dome on the 1781 Custom
House (now destroyed) he left behind in Dublin. Bulfinch's dome of
1798 on the Massachusetts State
House is also mentioned as inspiration. In 1836 James C. Bucklin
(1801–80) almost totally remodeled
the church. Bucklin, born in Providence, was probably Rhode Island's
most distinguished architect of the
nineteenth century, his most noted
building being the Providence Ar-
cade of 1829. The now well-
restored church (1987) has today an
outreach with an active Chinese-
American congregation and a bilin-
gual ministry. As the National Register of Historic Places sums up the
church's architecture: "Influential in
mid-19th C. development of surrounding commercial and residential
area."

89

FIRST UNITARIAN CHURCH [1816]

Benefit Street at Benevolent
Providence

John Holden Greene, architect

First Unitarian is one of the most precocious churches for its time in New England. Few houses of worship of the first years of the nineteenth century can match it for ambition, few can equal it for achievement. Though English developments were of influence, Greene—born in nearby Warwick—carried his design through with panache. The dramatic scale of the facade with its flamboyantly detailed gigantic broken pediment, round-headed "Gothic" window, and colossal columns set the scene. This is capped by a square tower with its own broken pediments, surmounted by a wondrous octagonal belfry and topped by an equally extraordinary lantern, with small stage and spire above, all displaying almost uninhibited flair. Two-story round-headed windows also appear in the white local stone sides and east end of the church.

The light, lofty auditorium forms a squarish room of unusual breadth and height (antithesis to the long naves of the Church of England), knit together by a wide-embracing saucer dome from which depends a crystal chandelier (replaced in 1916).

Four huge Corinthian columns, one per corner, support the nave side of the stepped galleries. Virtually the only liturgical element is a handsome, raised mahogany pulpit with a plain marble slab below serving as an altar. Clergy access doors on either side and a finely detailed "panel" above the altar, the panel's round head echoing the windows on either side, lend emphasis to the pulpit.

The usual "improvements" via stenciled decorations and painted glass were applied in the 1860s but removed in 1916. A fire, started by lightning, caused serious damage in 1966 but the church's thick stone walls and heavy wood beams prevented structural damage. Originally known as the First Congregational Church, its name was changed to the First Unitarian Church of Providence in 1953. Its architecture displays the "lavish Late Colonial" at its best (Talbot Hamlin, *Greek Revival Architecture in America,* Oxford University Press, 1944).

The hillside area surrounding the church contains a comely collection of largely unspoiled houses and other buildings from the eighteenth almost through the nineteenth centuries: they are well worth exploring.

90

GRACE CHURCH [1846]

175 Mathewson Street at
  Westminster Mall
Providence

Richard Upjohn, architect

Richard Upjohn, the most important ecclesiastic architect of the mid and late nineteenth century, was very active in Rhode Island (see his Church of the Holy Cross in Middletown-Newport; 83), and this 1846 effort might be termed a typical old-line mid-city Episcopal church of its era. In spite of being gruffly hemmed in by today's structures and aggravated by traffic (the area was once residential) Grace Church carries on actively. Measuring 82 feet/25 m wide by 147 feet/45 m long it is built of reddish stone laid in ashlar pattern, and possesses unusual unity and compactness. The stone of the walls and the well-buttressed tower continues in the tall louvered belfry and spire (1860), completing its homogeneity. Its corner tower (instead of being on axis) acts as an urban pivot at 206 feet/62 m in height. Note the double angle of the roof planes marking the side aisles.

The interior maintains the Gothic Revival spirit of the exterior: no lateral galleries, prominent wood trusses upholding the roof, Victorian windows (largely 1890s), low (too low) level of natural light, and prominent chancel. The chancel end was extended and substantially altered in 1912 by Cram, Goodhue & Ferguson, the distinguished firm that did so much early twentieth-century work.

Note: Upjohn used a similar Gothic Revival style for St. Stephen's Church (1862) at 114 George Street also in Providence.

A simple but elegant church, also
known as St. Paul's Episcopal,
which reveals expertise through proportion and detail. It occupies a bucolic setting on the edge of town and
is surrounded by a respectful cemetery. The building's plain rectangular
shape is topped by a gable roof that
accents the basic geometry of its
form. The only decorative features
of the exterior are the round-headed
windows of the lower rank (note the
arched panes) plus a magnificent
double door framed by Tuscan pilasters and topped by a boldly handsome broken-arched pediment. In
1811 a steeple was attached to the
east end but collapsed in 1866 and
was never replaced. The upper windows are flat and abut the eaves.

The plan is probably unique in the
Episcopal Church in having the entry on the long side facing the pulpit
(on north wall) in meetinghouse
fashion. The octagonal pulpit rises
above the lectern—both smartly
paneled—but there is glare from the
two windows directly behind. The
overall interior setting is on the spartan side, as would be expected from
its early date. The galleries were
added in 1723. The building was
moved some 5 miles/8 km to its
present site in 1800, reflecting population changes occasioned by the
Revolution. In time deserted and
suffering abuse, the church—among
the oldest Episcopal churches in the
country—was beautifully restored
outside and in in the 1920s by Nor-
man M. Isham.

91

OLD NARRAGANSETT CHURCH
[1707]

60 Church Lane (1 block north of
   Main)
Wickford (North Kingstown)

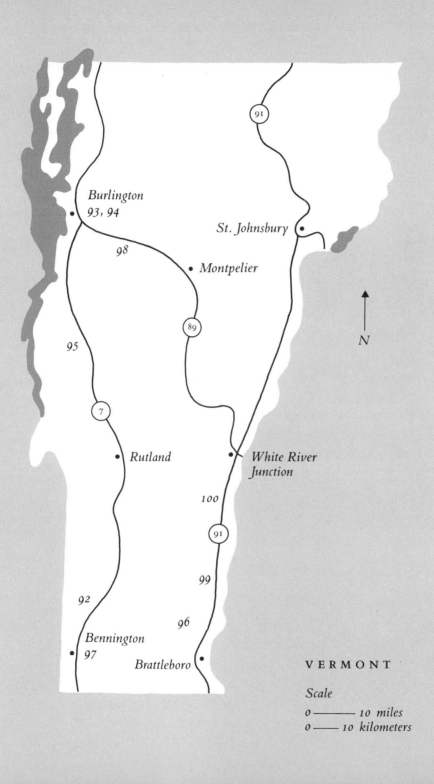

Burlington
93, 94

St. Johnsbury

98

Montpelier

89

95

7

Rutland

White River
Junction

100

91

99

92

96

Bennington
97

Brattleboro

N

VERMONT

Scale
0 ——— 10 miles
0 ——— 10 kilometers

ST. JAMES EPISCOPAL CHURCH
[1831]

Main Street/VT 7A
Arlington

William Passman, architect

Arlington, a dozen or so miles (20 km) north of Bennington, still maintains its village charm, being fortunately bypassed by the main highway to the east. St. James—an Episcopal stranger amidst Congregationalists—replaces a wooden church which had burned. Its design is basically Gothic Revival and, as Professor William H. Pierson perceptively points out in volume 2 of his *American Buildings and Their Architects,* its exterior recalls Trinity Church in New Haven, Connecticut (16) and St. Paul's (Troy, New York). The rectangular body of the church is of stone, three to four feet thick, with a fanciful wood tower rising straight from the projected stone entry. Wood "tracery" decorates both the tower and its belfry with an array of eight finials prancing on top. The semiarched front door is juxtaposed by elongated lancet windows on either side with a squarish window above the entry.

The surprisingly lofty interior is crowned by three pointed vaults upheld in the nave by attenuated quadrifoil wood columns. The chancel is unusual in having a modest rood screen. The stained glass in the sanctuary wall—depicting St. James—dates from the end of the last century as does the routine glass in the nave.

Of architect William Passman little is known. Reputedly he came from England and, it is thought, returned there after finishing this church. (See William H. Pierson, Jr.'s encyclopedic *American Buildings and Their Architects* [Doubleday, 1978]).

The "Olde Burying Ground," tracing the church's founding to the mid eighteenth century, lies adjacent.

Within sight of Lake Champlain and anchoring a downtown area stabilized by National Historic designation, First Unitarian—the oldest church in the city—is an impressive achievement particularly in that the town had scarce 2,000 souls when it was built. Today it is hemmed in by automobiles and commerce, but holds down the street with kindly authority as the focus of Burlington (now 38,000). It was designed by the English-born and educated Peter Banner, who early moved to America and worked largely in the Federal Style of sharp-edged red brick forms with white trim so popular in the new country in the early 1800s. First Unitarian is the tidy result. Its projected square brick tower with delicate wood balustrade is well tied to the mass of the building and is topped by a competent octagonal open belfry and a lantern with spire rising above. In 1955 lightning struck the steeple, necessitating its complete replacement; the whole city, irrespective of faith, responded to meet the cost. Almost unbelievably, the architect's original drawings were found in the Archives of the Library of Congress in Washington.

The oft-changed interior—updated "according to the taste of the times" (1845)—forms a well-lit worship space with the usual balconies on three sides. Four of the roof timbers are 61.5 feet/18.6 m long! The pulpit wall originally had four windows but these were closed when the parish house addition was made (1868). Thus what we see today, though pleasant in its simplicity, is not the design of the talented Mr. Banner.

The "Head of Church Street Historic District" rewards a stroll.

93

FIRST UNITARIAN UNIVERSALIST SOCIETY [1817]

141 Church Street at Pearl
Burlington

Peter Banner, architect

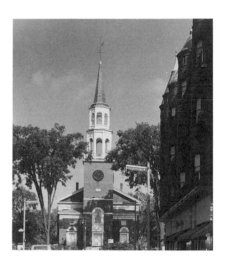

94

CATHEDRAL OF THE IMMACULATE
CONCEPTION [1977]

Pine Street between Cherry and
  Pearl
Burlington

Edward Larrabee Barnes, architect

The problem of designing a church for today's uneasy ethos, especially a downtown church in the moil of commercialism, involves both a religious response of positiveness and an urban solution of identity. Architect Barnes has solved these interlocked problems with comeliness and grace. Occupying much of a city block, the cathedral—replacing one which burned in 1972—is set back in a grove of 120 locust trees which frame it on three sides. Behind this "insulation" rises the church, not as an abrupt affront to the neighborhood, but eased by angled profile which begins with a low belt of green and brown glazed brick and climaxes in a raised-seam copper roof. This powerful windowless geometry comprises three metallic planes at 40°, flexed vertically to contain the skylight which runs the axis of the church. The progression from low outer wall to the cross at top—the urban contour—is excellent.

The interior includes a rectangular main worship space, accommodating 284 in seven semicircular rows of fixed pews, and the small St. Patrick Chapel behind the sanctuary. A simple free-standing altar, with reredos containing a handsome boxed organ, establishes a spatial pivot between the two congregational areas. A full-length skylight (the nave has no other natural illumination) pours forth from 60 feet/18 m above, dramatically intensifying the great planes of the roof. The low ancillary worship space, triangular in plan, is lit by ten splayed lunettes set in the outer wall and producing a ring of light. Their half-round shape is echoed by the cylindrical light fixtures in the nave. They also might be said to pay faint homage to H. H. Richardson's Billings Student Center at the nearby University of Vermont. The large Greek cross window over the entry to the nave, made up of several shades of blue, was designed by Robert Sowers; the glass in the lunettes is by David Wilson. Mary Barnes and Toshiko Mori did the interior design. The free-standing steel bell tower outside is first-rate.

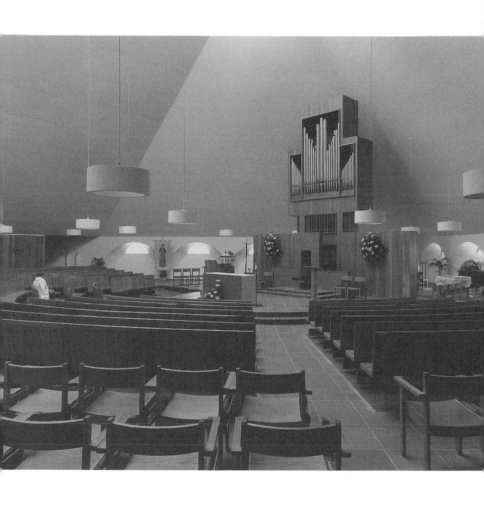

95

CONGREGATIONAL CHURCH
[1809]

The Common/US 7
Middlebury

Lavius Fillmore, architect

Though the Connecticut-born Fillmore (1767–1846) has been little noted in books on the development of architecture in the United States, he produced in Vermont two exceptional—and similar—churches. This at Middlebury was completed in 1809, four years after his pioneering effort in Old Bennington (97) 89 miles/143 km to the south. As such it shows greater sophistication in the design of the facade, while the interiors are basically alike.

The Middlebury church is lacerated by today's traffic and cut off from the small park in front: though semi-isolated it stands with commanding conviction. The relation of the projected front, with its sharply detailed entries and Palladian window, to the pediment and to the half-inset tower represents exceptional handling. This continues in the square belfry whose central arched opening is framed by pilasters and "blind niches" that recall the round tops of the flanking entry doors below. The stage above (with over-scaled clock) is topped by two richly detailed octagons, with spire rising 135 feet/41 m to be crowned by the usual weather vane.

The interior, which seats 725, is full of the architect's joy of light, but lacks the transcendent unity of his Old Bennington prototype to which it is structurally akin. (The Palladian window was restored in 1925, having earlier [1854] been walled up; other interior changes were made as recently as 1976.) Fine inside, Middlebury Congregational is magnificent on the exterior.

As with most New England churches of the early nineteenth century, indeed all building types of that era, there are design influences from available handbooks. These handbooks were highly popular because the developing United States had few skilled architects. The Englishman James Gibbs, a pupil of Christopher Wren, wrote the widely circulated *A Book of Architecture* (1728), while Massachusetts-born Asher Benjamin's *The Country Builder's Assistant* (1797) went through many editions. Fillmore used these books, but his Middlebury church makes many contributions of its own.

The church became part of the United Church of Christ in 1961. Incidentally, church and state in Vermont were separated in 1807.

96

FIRST CONGREGATIONAL CHURCH
[1839] AND VILLAGE

The Common
Main Street/VT 30
Newfane

There are two churches in the Newfane Village Historic District but
they are subsumed in the overall
statement of this unspoiled, early
nineteenth-century, very New England settlement. The fetching fifty-
nine buildings of this ensemble—
now under National Register protection—focus on the Common (alas,
bisected by Main Street). The Common in turn bows to the elegance of
its Windham County Court House,
whose capable Greek Revival tetra-
style temple front was added in 1853
to the 1825 body of the two-story
building.

Loosely nodding to the courthouse
are the two churches mentioned, of
which First Congregational on
Church Street is the only one still
active. Built in 1839, it was "modernized" later in the century as can
be seen in its "Gothic" pointed arch
shutters which are, it is interesting to
note, simply attached on the outside
with the regular windows behind.
The nearby and slightly earlier
Union Church—now Union Hall—
was built in 1832 and possibly was
the local forerunner of the vogue for
metamorphosing the Greek Revival
into the more "up-to-date" Gothic.

In the middle of the last century, reflecting Newfane's decline after the
Civil War, the congregation left—
many going west—and in 1872 the
building was converted into a public
hall.

The relaxed disposition of the
courthouse and churches, each of
which faces east toward Main Street,
finds cohesion in abundant trees and
greenery with a Civil War Memorial
and fountain providing accents. Two
recommended inns stand nearby.
West Street branches off the Common to northwest, unfolding a parade of Federal and Colonial Revival
private houses. Many of the village's
earliest structures originally stood
some two miles west in the high
hills (for water-power utilization),
and were moved by ox-cart and
sleds to the valley floor when the
courthouse was constructed.

The extraordinary homogeneity of
Newfane's buildings—their domestic
scale, white-painted clapboard sides,
and respectful spacing—make this
little-altered village (population ca.
1,200) unique.

97

FIRST CONGREGATIONAL CHURCH
[1806]

West end of Main Street/VT 9
Old Bennington

Lavius Fillmore, architect

The immediate delight of Old First
Church lies in its hilltop, tree-lined
setting which flows into the adjacent
cemetery (and wherein Robert Frost
lies buried); its secondary reward can
be found in its luminescent interior.
Its architect, Lavius Fillmore, a
cousin of the thirteenth president,
was one of the little-known but distinguished church designers of the
early nineteenth century, an uneasy
period politically and architecturally
following the Revolution. (See also
Fillmore's church at Middlebury; 95)
Historically, Old First, to use its
original name, had been "gathered"
in 1762 when Vermont was under
New Hampshire's aegis, and its first
building was a primitive pine meetinghouse used both for public gath-
erings and for worship. With state
identity and growing prosperity
marking the dawn of the new century, First Congregational was com-
missioned, "the first church built in
Vermont that reflects the separation
of church and state" (church bulletin). Its Federal style design, as the
bulletin also mentions, was based on
plate 33 of Asher Benjamin's widely
circulated *The Country Builder's Assistant,* but Fillmore went far beyond, particularly on the interior.

The projected front of the church is accented by three doors, the center one with pediment, the two adjacent round-headed, with a strong Palladian window above. A second Palladian window appears in the tower. (Andrea Palladio, who was born in Italy in 1508 and died there in 1580, was probably influential in the design of more buildings than any architect in history: his famous window with arched central section flanked by two shorter ones with flat heads was last seen illuminating a 1980s skyscraper in Boston. Palladio himself almost never used this design motif for a window.) Above rises an open octagonal belfry, a lantern with ovoid windows, cupola, and weather vane.

The interior has a quality of wholeness and of luminosity rarely seen in any church of any period. There are ten windows per side: the five in the balcony are round-headed to reflect the groined vaulting, while those below are square-headed. All have inside shutters which act as unexpected wings to reflect winter's sunshine and keep out summer's. The imposing pulpit, properly raised to survey the balconies, is more than well illuminated by another large Palladian window directly behind. The shallow circular dome over the nave is set within a lightly framed cruciform and is partially supported by double-height Ionic columns. The gallery sweeps around the entry end of the nave in a half-circle, picking up the curves of windows and shutters. The forty-eight box pews add much to the geometric interlace of the interior. A sparkling chandelier (reproduced) hangs from the dome to give light and spatial accent. Altered and "modernized" four times in the nineteenth century—deplorably in 1865—the interior was fully restored in 1935–37.

98

OLD ROUND CHURCH [1813]

Off Exit 11 of IS 89, on Bridge
Street
Richmond

William Rhodes, designer

On the Euclidian thesis that a circle
can enclose maximum area per
length of perimeter, Rhodes—here
constrained by straight-stick lumber—designed this small sixteen-
sided meetinghouse/church for five
ecumenically minded Protestant
sects. Its sturdily profiled form, approximately 50 feet/15 m in diameter, culminates in an octagonal tower
with a stretched belfry and small
dome. Three doors on the cardinal
points give access, while dark windows on two levels punctuate the
white clapboard sides. The bright interior (which can be peeked at) has
box pews facing the raised pulpit
with gallery above, its supports
made from single pine trees. In the
middle of the nineteenth century
several sects left Old Round to establish churches of their own and its
religious use phased out. Town
meetings, however, have been held
here since 1880. It was fully restored
in 1973. Old Round is more of an
architectural curiosity than an architectural gem but the short trip from
Burlington, a dozen or so miles (20
km) to the west, will prove worth-
while. It is generally open in summer on Saturdays and Sundays.

99

OLD MEETINGHOUSE [1787]

Off VT 103, 1.4 mi/2 km northwest
of Exit 6 of IS 91
Rockingham

The Rockingham Meetinghouse/First Church, presiding over the countryside from its hilltop site and surrounded on three sides by a fascinating variety of tombs, epitomizes late eighteenth-century religious architecture in New England. Its splendid—and defensible—location and its prismatic spireless form etched by white clapboards give it a no-nonsense conviction which has few equals. The spartan interior, now properly restored, is divided into a crosshatch of box pews each topped by a spindled railing. These "pigpen" pews held from ten to fifteen worshipers each and were reached by aisles known as "alleys." A long narrow pew for church officers stretches in front of the pulpit. The usual three-sided gallery occupies the upper level; total capacity is reportedly almost a thousand. The wall behind the pulpit might be said to constitute an exercise in visual flagellation with twelve 6-foot/1.8 m-high windows of forty panes each glaring at the congregation, while the outsize round-headed window behind the handsome pulpit tends to silhouette the preacher.

Religious services were phased out by 1839, many denominations erecting their own church, and town meetings were moved in 1869 to nearby and more prosperous Bellows Falls. The building, which measures 56 by 44 feet/17 by 13 m, was virtually abandoned and partially vandalized but in 1907, following meticulous restoration (including 1,400 pew-top spindles), it was rededicated on its 120th birthday. Since then it has been proudly maintained by the Old Rockingham Meeting House Association. One of the greats.

100

OLD SOUTH CHURCH [1798]

Main Street/US 5
Windsor

Asher Benjamin, architect

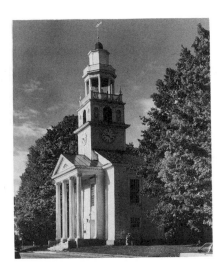

Windsor is the earliest town in Vermont's history, for it was here along the Connecticut River that in 1777 the state was officially "born" and named. Moreover, it was the first state to outlaw slavery, though it did not join the Union until 1791 because of land disagreements with New York. The town's imposing Old South Church—earlier known as South Meeting House—rises directly from the main street. Its freestanding porch is upheld by four attenuated Ionic columns and gives shelter to the twin entries. The first stage of the tower is unusual with its louvers and richly decorated niches containing urns. Above, behind a balustrade, is a lofty open octagonal belfry, with simple stage and low dome atop. Altogether a sturdy profile.

The two stories of the church are divided into a low ground floor used for general parish functions and a large worship room above. The auditorium is introduced by a foyer with a Tiffany window. The late nineteenth-century "Victorian" stained glass of the nave is an anachronism in its eighteenth-century frame but the overall atmosphere is cheerful. Old South, like many New England churches in the mid nineteenth century, underwent drastic changes: its "noble interior was completely ruined in 1844 by 'improvements,' " while in 1879 "the auditorium was completely gone over" (again). However, in 1923 it was happily returned "to its original Colonial style of architecture" (church bulletin.)

Take a look, also, at the ancient cemetery which surrounds the church on three sides and is well worth exploring.

GLOSSARY, CHRONOLOGY, AND INDEXES

Architrave	The trim around a door or window. In classic architecture the bottom third of the horizontal members which rest directly on columns.
Ashlar masonry	Stone cut in rectangles—smooth or rough, aligned or random.
Baldachino	A protective covering or canopy over an altar. Also called a ciborium.
Balustrade	A safety or decorative railing around a stair or atop a building.
Barge board	A scroll-cut decorative board at edge of gable, mostly nineteenth century.
Belt course	A flat horizontal band of small projection marking a facade division. Also called a string course.
Betonglas	Thick (1 inch/2.5 cm) glass faceted on one side.
Board and batten	Vertical wood siding whose joints are covered by narrow strips or battens.
Box pews	Seventeenth- and eighteenth-century squarish enclosed pews generally "owned" by families; high-backed against drafts in heatless churches.
Chancel	The main (generally east) end of a church: the part reserved for altar, clergy, and choir.
Clerestory	The topmost windows in the nave of a church: any high band of windows.

Corinthian Order	The richest of the Greek and Roman orders, its capitals representing stylized acanthus leaves.
Cornice	The projecting eave atop a building; also the top section of an entablature outside or in.
Cruciform plan	Longitudinal (Gothic) church plan with long nave, transepts, and chancel.
Cupola	A small domed accent atop a steeple.
Dentils	A line of small decorative blocks in the cornice of a classical molding.
Doric Order	The oldest and simplest of the three Classical orders. The Greek Doric is fluted and has no base.
Entablature	The horizontal group of members of Classic architecture which rests directly on the columns. It is divided into architrave (at bottom), frieze, and cornice, the last directly under roof overhang.
Entasis	The slightly swelling profile curve of a Greek or Roman column.
Facade	The front or face of a building, usually the main elevation.
Federal Style	The post-Revolution architectural style in America, lasting roughly to the 1830s. Planar and restrained, it achieved great elegance.
Fenestration	The disposition of windows in a facade.
Frieze	The middle member of the three-part entablature: architrave, frieze, cornice. It was often decorated in Greek order with triglyphs and metopes.
Gable	The triangular, upper end of a building framed by the two roof planes.
Galleries	A partial upper floor with seating generally on three sides. A balcony.
Gambrel roof	A roof with two slopes (instead of one) on each of its long sides, the lower sharply pitched.
Georgian architecture	The rich, basically symmetrical style of architecture of much of the eighteenth century, epitomized by Williamsburg.

Gothic Revival	A period in architecture which sought to revive the medieval Gothic for houses of worship. Popular in the United States from the early 1800s.
Greek-cross plan	A church plan with four equal-length arms.
Greek Revival	A style based on Classical Greek prototypes or details, popular in the United States 1820–50.
Groined vaults	The intersection of two vaults at right angles.
Hip roof	A roof with four planes sloping from the horizontal ridge.
Ionic Order	One of the three major Classical orders: its capitals are identified by volutes.
Lancet window	A window with sharply arched head. Gothic-inspired.
Lantern	A small decorative superstructure on a steeple, usually glazed, and with cupola and spire on top.
Lintel	A beam over an opening or resting on two supports: post-and-lintel construction.
Metopes	The small panels in a Doric frieze between the triglyphs. Often sculpted.
Modillions	Ornamental scroll brackets under an eave in the Greek Corinthian order.
Ogee arch	An arch with a double curve ending in a point.
Palladian window	A tripartite window with tall arched central sections flanked by lower flat-headed side windows. Named for the Italian architect Andrea Palladio (1508–80).
Pediment	The triangular space of a gable-ended building. Also used on a small scale over doors and windows in triangular, segmental (arched), and "broken" form.
Pilaster	A thin rectangular "column" used to establish wall divisions.
Plinth	A square block supporting a column or statue.
Purlin	A secondary horizontal beam used in trusses to support roof rafters.

Rafters	The framing members, generally angled, which support the roof.
Reredos	An ornamental screen behind the altar.
Roundel	Small circular window or opening.
Segmental arch	A partial arch over a window.
Slip pews	Parallel pews as seen in today's churches: they replaced box pews (q.v.).
Sounding board	A voice reflector over a pulpit, often suspended.
Spire	The tapered top member of a steeple.
Steeple	A church tower and its spire.
String course	A simple band, usually found in brick buildings, stretching across a facade. Also called a belt course (q.v.).
Stylobate	The platform, generally of three steps in Classic architecture, on which rests the building.
Transepts	In a cruciform church the short side arms in front of the chancel and at right angles to the nave.
Triglyphs	The small vertically incised blocks in a Doric frieze.
Truss	A generally triangulated wood (or metal or concrete) frame used to span a space and support a (roof) load.
Tympanum	The inner triangle of a pediment.

1824 First United Church of Christ
Milford, Conn.; 13

1824 The First Church
Deerfield, Mass.; 47

1826 First Parish Church
Portland, Me.; 31

1826 Unitarian Universalist Church
Portsmouth, N.H.; 77

1827 First Congregational Church
Cheshire, Conn.; 3

1828 United First Parish Church
Quincy, Mass.; 55

1828 St. Andrew's Episcopal Church
Hopkinton, N.H.; 72

1829 First Congregational Church
Litchfield, Conn.; 9

1830 Center Congregational Church
Meriden, Conn.; 12

1830 First Chruch of Christ
Simsbury, Conn.; 20

1831 St. James Episcopal Church
Arlington, Vt.; 92

1832 Baptist Meetinghouse
Sturbridge, Mass.; 58

1838 First Congregational Church
Madison, Conn.; 11

1839 First Congregational Church
Newfane, Vt.; 96

1840/1909 First Congregational Church
Wicasset, Me.; 34

1842 Church
Temple, N.H.; 80

1843 Elijah Kellogg Church
Hapswell Center, Me.; 27

1844 Winter Street Church
Bath, Me.; 24

1845 Church of the Holy Cross
Middletown-Newport, R.I.; 83

1846 First Parish Church
Brunswick, Me.; 25

1846 Grace Church
Providence, R.I.; 90

1850 St. James
New London, Conn.; 17

1851 First Universalist Church
Provincetown, Mass.; 54

INDEX OF BUILDINGS

INDEX OF ARCHITECTS

INDEX OF DENOMINATIONS